THE LAW OF
THE WORKPLACE

Rights of
Employers and Employees

Second Edition

HE LAW OF
HE WORKPLACE

ights of
mployers and Employees

econd Edition

James W. Hunt

The Bureau of National Affairs Inc., Washington, D.C.

Copyright © 1984, 1988
The Bureau of National Affairs Inc.

Second Printing March 1989

Library of Congress Cataloging in Publication Data

Hunt, James W.
    The law of the workplace.

    Includes index.
  1. Labor laws and legislation—United States.
I. Title.
KF3319.H83 1984
ISBN 0-87179-574-4

International Standard Book Number: 0-87179-574-4
Printed in the United States of America

INTRODUCTION

More than 100 million Americans work for a living. Some are self-employed, but most work for others in offices, stores, schools, factories, mines, and other facilities.

While their jobs may differ, virtually all workers and their employers are directly affected by the laws that extend to all types of jobs and all aspects of employment and indeed affect most working men and women from the time before they are hired until after they retire.

More specifically, these work-related laws:

- Expand employment opportunities for job seekers through job training programs.
- Provide persons who are out of work with assistance in finding jobs.
- Regulate entry into certain occupations.
- Require nondiscriminatory hiring, pay, and other employment practices.
- Restrict the circumstances in which employees can be fired.
- Allow workers to join or form unions.
- Provide financial assistance to workers who lose their jobs or become disabled.
- Establish minimum wage rates and job safety standards.
- Regulate private pension plans and provide workers with a basic retirement income through Social Security.

Many employers and employees, however, are unfamiliar with the extent to which these laws affect their rights and responsibilities. There is also a lack of a government source for working people to contact for information about the overall scope of the laws and programs that affect them, largely because of the specialization of each of the federal and state agencies involved with employment-related matters.

The purpose of this book is to fill this informational gap for employers and employees by providing them with a summary of current workplace laws, the ways these laws affect them, and the agencies and programs involved.

These laws generally fall into one of two categories. The first covers on-the-job occurrences, such as employment discrimination, union activity, and safety practices.

Laws relating to these matters, and the regulations issued by government agencies, establish ground rules that govern the conduct and practices of employers, employees, and unions in the workplace. They are often enforced as adversary proceedings that start with a person charging an employer or a union with violating a law or regulation, followed by an investigation or hearing by an agency, and then a decision by the agency determining whether or not the alleged violation occurred, with the accused party being ordered to take corrective action if the agency finds that it did engage in prohibited conduct.

The other general category of employment law covers those programs providing services for persons seeking work, or benefits for former job holders, such as training for job seekers, and unemployment and Social Security benefits for the jobless, disabled, or retired worker.

These laws for the most part involve nonadversary proceedings: An individual files a claim or application with an administrative agency which then determines the person's entitlement to the requested service or benefit. Or, as discussed in Chapter 1, the agency's function may simply be one of providing basic information about job opportunities to a job seeker.

This book does not intend to make any claim to answer the vast number of legal questions that can arise relating to a person's job. Competent legal or other professional help should be sought for advice and guidance in specific situations.

CONTENTS

THE DEVELOPING LAW
OF THE WORKPLACE

Today's far-reaching workplace laws have their origin in federal and state labor laws dating back to the last century.

Indeed, the states, rather than the federal government, were the first to enact labor laws, starting with Massachusetts' 1836 statute regulating child labor. Massachusetts was also the first state to adopt a minimum wage law (1912). Wisconsin also had two "firsts": It was the first state to put into effect a workers' compensation program (1911), and the first to enact an unemployment insurance law (1932).

The federal government began enacting most of its labor laws in the last 50 years. These laws, referred to in this book, are listed below according to the year in which they became law. The title and section numbers of the U.S. Code containing these laws are also noted.

1883 Civil Service Act, 5 U.S.C. §2101

1926 Railway Labor Act, 45 U.S.C. §151

1935 Davis-Bacon Act, 40 U.S.C. §276a

1935 National Labor Relations Act, 29 U.S.C. §151
   (amended by the Labor Management Relations Act in 1947)

1936 Social Security Act, 42 U.S.C. §301

1938 Fair Labor Standards Act, 29 U.S.C. §201
   (amended by the Equal Pay Act in 1963)

1959 Labor Management Reporting and Disclosure Act, 29 U.S.C. §401

1962 Work Hours and Safety Act, 40 U.S.C. §327

1964 Title VII, 1964 Civil Rights Act, 42 U.S.C. §2000e

1965 McNamara-O'Hara Service Contract Act, 41 U.S.C. §351

1967 Age Discrimination in Employment Act, 29 U.S.C. §621

1970 Occupational Safety and Health Act, 29 U.S.C. §651

1972 Vietnam Era Veterans' Readjustment Assistance Act, 38 U.S.C. §2011

1973 Vocational Rehabilitation Act (handicapped employment amendment), 29 U.S.C. §793

1974 Employee Retirement Income Security Act, 29 U.S.C. §1001

1982 Job Training Partnership Act, U.S.C. §1501

1986 Immigration Reform and Control Act, 8 U.S.C. §1324a

This list, while current, is not complete. The laws of the workplace continue to evolve and develop. Each year federal and state legislators make changes to the laws, ranging from modifications of existing statutes, such as changes in the minimum wage, to the enactment of entirely new laws, such as those regulating smoking in the workplace. Still other areas are being considered by federal and state lawmakers as the subjects of proposed future legislation. Matters under consideration include proposals to allow workers to take extended parental leave and measures requiring mandatory health insurance for all employees. Rulings and decisions by administrative agencies and courts also frequently have a profound impact on the law.

Keeping current with these frequent changes is not always an easy task, but there are various sources available for this purpose. The publisher of this book, The Bureau of National Affairs, is one of several private companies providing up-to-date information on changes in workplace laws by legislators, agencies, and courts.

In addition, an excellent source of information on legislative activity in the states is the *Monthly Labor Review*, a publication of the U.S. Department of Labor. Its annual January issue contains a complete summary of the workplace laws enacted by state legislators in the preceding year. The *Monthly Labor Review* is available in most libraries.

ACRONYMS

AAP	Affirmative Action Program
AFDC	Aid to Families With Dependent Children
AFL-CIO	American Federation of Labor-Congress of Industrial Organizations
ALJ	Administrative Law Judge
BFOQ	Bona Fide Occupational Qualification
CETA	Comprehensive Employment and Training Act
CFR	Code of Federal Regulations
CLEP	College-Level Education Program
DHHS	Department of Health and Human Services
DIB	Disability Insurance Benefits
DOL	Department of Labor
DUA	Disaster Unemployment Assistance
EEO	Equal Employment Opportunity
EEOC	Equal Employment Opportunity Commission
EPA	Equal Pay Act
ERISA	Employee Retirement Income Security Act
ESA	Employment Standards Administration
ETA	Employment and Training Administration
FEP	Fair Employment Practices
FICA	Federal Insurance Contribution Act
FLRA	Federal Labor Relations Authority
FLSA	Fair Labor Standards Act
FMCS	Federal Mediation and Conciliation Service
GED	General Education Development
IRA	Individual Retirement Account
JTPA	Job Training Partnership Act
INS	Immigration and Naturalization Service
LMRDA	Labor Management Reporting and Disclosure Act
LMSA	Labor Management Services Administration
MSPB	Merit Systems Protection Board
NLRA	National Labor Relations Act
NLRB	National Labor Relations Board
NMB	National Mediation Board
OFCCP	Office of Federal Contract Compliance Programs
OPM	Office of Personnel Management
OSHA	Occupational Safety and Health Administration

OWCP   Office of Workers' Compensation Programs
RIB   Retirement Insurance Benefits
RIF   Reduction in Force
RLA   Railway Labor Act
SEP   Simplified Employee Pension Plan
SES   Senior Executive Service
SSA   Social Security Administration
SSI   Supplemental Security Income
TAA   Trade Adjustment Assistance Act
UC   Unemployment Compensation
UEP   Unfair Employment Practice
UI   Unemployment Insurance
ULP   Unfair Labor Practice
USES   U.S. Employment Service
WC   Workers' Compensation
WIN   Work Incentive Program

1
PROGRAMS FOR JOB SEEKERS

A basic requirement for getting a job is the ability to perform the work required. Although many entry-level positions require only that a person be able to perform simple tasks, greater qualifications are needed to advance to more responsible and better paid positions.

Most job training for these positions is provided by employers to those employees having the aptitude and willingness to do the work. But federal and state governments, often through joint efforts, also offer a variety of programs to equip both job holders and job seekers with the means to qualify for higher level positions.

Job Information Services

Many persons, whether young workers new to the labor market or experienced workers looking for a new line of work, are unfamiliar with the range of available career opportunities that they may be qualified to pursue with the necessary education and training. An information source that can help is the U.S. Department of Labor's *Occupational Outlook Handbook*, which describes different jobs, the education and training requirements needed for these jobs, expected earnings, and career potential in these positions.

The *Handbook* provides detailed information on more than 250 occupations—from production and service jobs to administrative, managerial, and professional positions—and lists the names and addresses of state agencies to contact for information about each state's job situation, as well as the names of public and private organizations covering a wide range of jobs and careers. Suggestions on how to look for a job are also included.

A related Labor Department publication, the *Dictionary of Occupational Titles*, while not providing the comprehensive job descriptions contained in the *Handbook*, does list the nearly 20,000 jobs that exist.

Most public libraries have the *Handbook* and the *Dictionary*. They can also be bought from:
U.S. Superintendent of Documents
Washington, D.C. 20402

U.S. Employment Service

The U.S. Employment Service, a federal-state system of more than 1,700 local Job Service offices nationwide, offers "no fee" assistance to all job seekers and employers who ask for it. Local Job Service offices, through a job matching system that is computerized in many cities, provide up-to-date information on jobs currently in demand, from entry-level positions to technical and professional occupations, and information on where such jobs are located, the training needed, and their rates of pay. In some instances even out-of-state jobs are listed.

The Job Service also helps employers obtain workers for their general work force as well as for jobs requiring special skills and experience. The Job Service is listed in the telephone directory under that name, or as the Employment Security Commission, or Employment Service, depending on what each state calls its service. A Job Service office can also provide information on the training programs referred to in this chapter.

Education Assistance

In today's competitive labor market the lack of a high school diploma or college degree can frustrate the career advancement of many otherwise qualified workers. Therefore, local school systems have developed programs for working adults to give them the opportunity to obtain the formal educational qualifications they lack without spending long hours in the classroom. Some programs, for example, allow adults to earn high school equivalency certificates through the General Educational Development (GED) program, while college credit can be obtained through such systems as the College-Level Education Program (CLEP). More information about these and other programs can be obtained through a local school system or by writing to:

GED Testing Service   CLEP College Board
One Dupont Circle, N.W.   Department C
Washington, D.C. 20036   88 7th Avenue
                             New York, N.Y. 10019

Apprenticeships

Apprenticeship programs operated under federally approved standards provide combined on-the-job and classroom training to persons learning to perform the work of a highly skilled occupation, such as automotive mechanic, electrician, or carpenter. There are literally hundreds of apprenticeship trades, with the training lasting from one to six years, depending on the trade, until the worker becomes a full-fledged journeyman.

The programs are usually employer-sponsored, with many co-sponsored by labor unions. Qualifications generally require that an applicant be at least 16 years old and have a high school diploma or GED certificate. The programs must be open to both men and women. Some receive government funding and many are operated in correctional institutions to provide inmates with a legitimate trade they can practice upon their release.

National standards governing the scope of the training, instruction, and pay are approved by the federal government's Bureau of Apprenticeship and Training or by a state apprenticeship council.

For more information, contact a local Job Service office or write to:

Bureau of Apprenticeship and Training
U.S. Department of Labor
601 D Street, N.W.
Washington, D.C. 20213

Youth Programs

Under the federal Job Corps program, disadvantaged youths aged 16—21 are provided with a broad range of work experience, training, and services, including basic education and health services, to enhance their employability in what job specialists call the "world of work." The services are provided through full-time residential centers. Other youth programs include short-term summer employment for disadvantaged young people.

Work Incentive Program

Persons 16 years of age or older who receive or apply for Aid to Families with Dependent Children are required to register for the Work Incentive (WIN) program at a local Job Service office. The WIN program, operated jointly by the U.S. Departments of Labor and Health and Human Services, provides various services to the registrants to help them find and hold jobs.

Job Training Partnership Act

The Job Training Partnership Act (JTPA) provides job training and assistance for economically disadvantaged youth and adults to assist their entry into the labor market. It also provides training and other employment services to dislocated workers—those laid off due to plant closings, the long-term unemployed, and those unable to return to the same industry or occupation. State governments provide matching funds for the programs for dislocated workers.

Under JTPA the governors of each state designate Service Delivery Areas (SDAs) within their states where local government units and Private Industry Councils (PICs) develop job training plans tailored to their areas. SDAs can be composed of one or more cities or counties, while PICs are made up mostly from representatives from private industry, together with representatives from labor unions and other community-based organizations. JTPA employment programs are also coordinated with the local Job Service.

Rehabilitation Services for Handicapped Persons

A federal-state system of local vocational rehabilitation agencies provides services to persons 16 years of age or older having a physical or mental disability that hinders their ability to find work. Rehabilitation services, which are provided if the individual can reasonably be expected to benefit from them, are tailored to the individual and can include corrective surgery, artificial limbs, transportation to receive services, education, on-the-job training, vocational training, and counseling.

Federal law also reserves the opportunity for the blind to run vending facilities in federal buildings, and employers with workshop programs providing training and jobs for blind and handicapped individuals receive preference in bidding on government contracts for products and services.

Bonding Program

Some employers require that their employees be bonded, a form of insurance protecting the employer against employee dishonesty, theft, or embezzlement. Insurance companies, however, often refuse to bond individuals with a criminal record, a history of alcohol or drug abuse, or a poor credit record. These persons consequently are not hired when a bond is required even though they may have been rehabilitated. Under the federal bonding program a person not commercially bondable because of one of the above reasons, but otherwise qualified for an available job, can apply for and receive a bond at a Job Service office.

Other Programs

Somewhat lower on the scale than the others, but nevertheless important to the persons they serve, are programs for older workers, native Americans, and migrant workers. As with most government-sponsored programs, the Job Service is the agency to contact for information.

There are, of course, many nongovernmental, privately operated programs providing training for occupations ranging from secretarial positions to truck driver and computer operator. And there are also private job counseling and placement agencies. Like the government-sponsored employment programs, private sector activities serve job seekers by providing them with the qualifications and assistance needed to get hired for, and advance in, the jobs they want.

In 44 states private employment agencies are regulated by laws that generally limit the fees that agencies can charge for their services.

Tax Credits

Although not a program as such, employers hiring workers from specified "target" groups can receive a tax credit of up to $3,000 for each person they hire. There are 10 target groups, including:

- Welfare recipients;
- Handicapped persons;
- Young workers (14—18 years old) from economically disadvantaged families;
- Economically disadvantaged Vietnam-era veterans; and
- Economically disadvantaged ex-offenders.

An employer interested in obtaining a tax credit can contact a local Internal Revenue Service office for more information.

Workers are also allowed tax credits for the actual expense incurred for child or dependent care, including care for a dependent spouse who is physically or mentally unable to care for himself or herself, when the expense is necessary to enable the worker to be gainfully employed. The credit is 30 percent for taxpayers with incomes of $10,000 or less with a reduction in the credit for workers with larger incomes. More information about the credit is provided in the instructions the IRS sends to individual taxpayers with their tax forms.

EMPLOYEE TAX DEDUCTIONS

An employee who itemizes deductions on his or her federal income tax return is allowed to deduct certain employment-related expenses, but only to the extent that the employee was not reimbursed for the expense. These deductions include:

- Moving costs if there was a change in the employee's job location of at least 35 miles from the old residence to the place of work;
- Expenses for business travel, transportation (but not commuting expenses to and from work), meals and lodging;
- Union or professional dues;
- Tools, employer-required uniforms, and safety equipment used in the employee's work;
- Costs for education required by the employer, or by law or regulation, in order to keep a present job or salary;
- Physical examinations required by the employer; and
- Fees paid to employment agencies and other costs to get a new job in the employee's present trade or profession.

Either a local office of the Internal Revenue Service or a public library has publications explaining these deductions in more detail.

2

EMPLOYMENT RESTRICTIONS

Americans have a basic right to pursue any legitimate business, occupation, or profession as a means of earning a living. The laws of state and federal governments, as indicated in the last chapter, have generally been intended to promote that right by expanding job opportunities through various employment services.

A government, however, also has the power to impose in the public's interest reasonable restrictions on an individual's right to operate a business or perform some types or work. When this power has been exercised, it has been used to place restrictions on the employment of women, ex-offenders, children, and aliens. It has also been used to restrict entry by all persons into certain jobs through occupational licensing laws.

State Protective Laws

Many states in the past adopted laws to protect women from the hazards of industrial work by restricting the type of work they could perform, the number of hours they could work, night-work, and the maximum weight they could be required to lift.

These laws, however, are now generally considered to limit job opportunities for women rather than protecting them. Although they are still on the books in some states, the federal Equal Employment Opportunity Commission, which enforces the law prohibiting job discrimination, does not consider an employer's reliance on such laws in denying a woman a job to be a valid defense to a charge of unlawful sex discrimination.

Occupational Licensing

Occupational licensing is in effect permission from a government-created board or commission to engage in some job, trade, or profession. All states have enacted laws that make it illegal for an unlicensed person to work in an occupation that requires government licensure or certification. The basis for the government's licensing authority is that certain jobs affect the public in such a way that the government can require that persons wanting to work in these jobs have a minimum level of competency in order to protect the public's health, safety, and welfare.

The occupations regulated by licensing laws vary from state to state and cover a variety of vocations, trades, and professions, ranging from, in some states, fortune-teller and junk dealer, to, in all states, doctors, lawyers, and teachers. Some jobs, such as taxicab operator, are licensed by cities. Nationwide, more than seven million persons work in occupations or for businesses requiring a government license or certification.

Information about a state's occupational licensing requirements can be obtained from the licensing agencies listed in the telephone directory under the state government listing.

Ex-Offenders

The occupational licensing laws of some states expressly prohibit the issuance of a license to a person with a criminal record, while others contain indirect restrictions, such as the requirement that an applicant for a license be of "good moral character," which has often been used to exclude anyone with a police record. Some state laws also prohibit the employment of ex-felons in state jobs.

In recent years, however, about half the states have adopted laws which provide that an ex-offender is not to be automatically denied a license or a government job and that, in determining the applicant's fitness for a job or a license, consideration be given to the nature of the crime, its relation to the job the individual wants to perform, and his or her rehabilitation efforts.

The federal government applies essentially the same standards in considering whether ex-offenders applying for civil service jobs should be hired. Federal law, however, also prohibits persons convicted of certain offenses from holding office in a labor union and indirectly limits jobs and job training for offenders by prohibiting goods made in prison from being shipped across state lines or from being used on federally funded highway projects.

Young Workers

All states and the federal government have adopted child labor laws restricting the types and hours of work for young workers. These laws generally require that young workers obtain work permits from their local school system and that employers hiring young people observe the following standards:

- An 18-year minimum age for hazardous work;
- A 16-year minimum age for factory work;
- A 14-year minimum age for nonfactory work outside school hours (except for work on farms and such work as delivering newspapers);
- A maximum 40-hour work week for children under 16 years of age;

- Limitations on working time outside school hours for youth still in school (the limitations vary from state to state); and

- Restrictions on working at night.

More information about a state's child labor laws can be obtained from the state's labor department. The addresses of these departments are listed in Appendix A. Chapter 7 covers in more detail the federal child labor law.

Aliens

Aliens living in the United States do not have the right to work while here unless they fall into one of the categories of aliens allowed to work by the federal Immigration and Nationality Act. Indeed, it is unlawful for an employer to hire an alien who lacks authorization to work. The employer may be fined up to $2,000 if it does.

Aliens allowed by law to work include lawful permanent resident aliens and political refugees. Other aliens who are lawfully admitted into this country including non-immigrant students studying at American schools and relatives of foreign officials, must obtain authorization to work from the Immigration and Naturalization Service.

Other foreign workers may also be allowed to work temporarily or permanently in the United States, but only if qualified Americans are not available to do the work and the terms of employment for the foreign workers will not adversely affect the wages and working conditions of American workers. The conditions under which foreign workers are allowed to work depend on whether temporary or permanent work is sought.

Temporary employment. An employer, or his agent, anticipating a labor shortage not caused by a strike or lockout may apply for a "temporary labor certificate" for temporary foreign workers (ETA form 575-B). The application, filed with the Job Service office serving the area where the work is to be performed, must, among other requirements, document the employer's attempt to recruit Americans and show that it made job offers to Americans without regard to their race, color, religion, sex, age, or nationality, including offers to handicapped workers qualified to perform the work.

The Job Service will then attempt to recruit Americans for the jobs. If all conditions are met and there are still no qualified Americans available, the employer may be allowed to hire foreign workers. However, they can perform only the work indicated in the application. The regulations for using temporary foreign workers are in 20 CFR 621 and 655.

Permanent employment. An employer may apply for a labor certification to allow an alien to work permanently in the United States. An alien may also apply. The application for permanent employment (ETA form 750) can be obtained from a Job Service office, which is also where an employer files the application. An alien, however, files the application with a U. S. Consular office if he or she is living abroad, or with an office of the Immigration and Naturalization Service if he or she is living in the United States. Both employers and aliens may have an agent do the filing for them.

The government has facilitated the process for obtaining permanent employment applications by preparing two lists of occupations, called Schedules A and B. Schedule A lists the occupations for which there are not a sufficient number of qualified American workers; Schedule B lists the jobs for which there are a sufficient number. Aliens can apply only for Schedule A jobs, while employers can apply to have an alien hired to do a job listed in either Schedule A or B. The regulations listing the occupations in these schedules are in 20 CFR 656.

An employer applying for an alien's certification for an occupation not listed in Schedule A must document its efforts to recruit Americans for the job. The Job Service will still conduct its own job search to try to fill the position with an American before approving the certification.

In the event an employer wants to hire an alien of "exceptional ability in the performing arts," it is permitted to reject applications for the job from Americans who are less qualified than the alien. The government, however, makes the final determination whether to grant any request for a certification to allow an alien to work here.

More information about the employment of aliens can be obtained from:

Division of Labor Certification
U.S. Employment Service
601 D St., N.W.
Washington, D.C. 20213

Undocumented aliens. It is unlawful for an employer to hire aliens lacking the necessary documentation showing that they are authorized to work. The documents that aliens can use for this purpose, and to prove their identity, include a United States passport, an Alien Registration Card with a photograph, or an unexpired foreign passport with attached employment authorization.

Although employers are required to verify an alien's employment authorization and are prohibited from hiring undocumented aliens, they are also prohibited by the Immigration Reform and Control Act of 1986 from discriminating in the hiring of aliens because of their national origin and discriminating against aliens because of their citizenship when they intend to become American citizens. A separate federal law, Title VII of the 1964 Civil Rights Act, also prohibits discrimination on the basis of national origin.

3
CREATING THE EMPLOYMENT RELATIONSHIP

Americans have a basic right to seek work. This does not, however, guarantee that all persons will find or be hired for the jobs they want. With the exceptions noted below, employers generally have the right to decide which applicants to hire, or to refuse to hire, as long as they do not discriminate on the basis of race or sex or one of the other grounds discussed in later chapters.

Most exceptions to the general rule that an employer can decide which employees to hire extend to certain categories of former employees. Workers whose employment was terminated because of federal military service or because of being called to active duty in the National Guard in some states have the right to be rehired. Employees who were unlawfully discharged from their jobs have the right to be reinstated, and striking employees have a preferential right to employment in circumstances covered later in the discussion on strikes.

Job seekers, on the other hand, have the right to refuse jobs they do not want, to refuse to work for an employer for whom they do not wish to work, and to quit jobs they do not like. Americans, for that matter, have the right not to work at all.

Unemployed workers, however, can lose their entitlement to benefits under an unemployment compensation program if they refuse to look for work or refuse to accept suitable job offers. And "workfare" programs in about three-fourths of the states condition the payment of welfare benefits to recipients on their performing or attempting to perform some work.

Work Eligibility

Although Americans have the right to seek work, they must, under the 1986 Immigration Reform and Control Act, demonstrate their work eligibility.

For an American citizen a Social Security card with accompanying verification of the person's identity, such as a driver's license containing a photograph, is generally sufficient to establish the person's work eligibility. The employer must receive this documentation within three days of the person's employment and then complete a form called "Employment Eligibility Verification." This form, shown here, is largely self-explanatory. The same form is also used when an employer hires an alien as covered in the preceding chapter.

Social Security Card

A Social Security card is obtained by applying for one at a local Social Security office. A copy of the applicant's birth certificate together with a document showing the person's identity must accompany the application. Beginning in 1987, a Social Security card must be obtained by age five for any person being claimed as a dependent by a taxpayer. The person to whom a card is issued will receive an exclusive lifetime Social Security number. This number will be used thereafter by the government to credit payments to the person's Social Security account and will also serve as an identification number for income tax purposes.

Employers and Employees

An employer-employee relationship is created when the job seeker agrees to work or perform services for pay for someone else. The agreement itself does not have to be actually expressed; it can be shown by the conduct of the parties indicating that one agrees to perform work for the other with the understanding that he or she will be paid for the work performed. This arrangement is legally a contract whether written or not and imposes certain duties on both the employer and the employee.

Duties of Employers and Employees

An employee has a duty to follow his or her employer's instructions, work diligently, be loyal, and perform work only for the employer during the hours of employment. Otherwise, the employee can have a second job ("moonlight"), or engage in self-employment, as long as it does not adversely affect the duties owed to the employer.

Any invention the employee develops on his or her own time belongs to the employee, unless there is an agreement to the contrary with the employer, or unless the employee was expressly hired to develop inventions. The employee, however, has no right to disclose secret processes or methods developed by the employer, even if the employee should leave the employer to work for someone else. The employee does, on the other hand, have the right to use the technical knowledge or skills in a new position that he or she learned in the prior job.

An employer, for its part, has a duty to an employee to:

- Pay for the work performed.
- Refrain from discriminating in pay, promotions, benefits, and working conditions because of the employee's race or

EMPLOYMENT ELIGIBILITY VERIFICATION (Form I-9)

1 **EMPLOYEE INFORMATION AND VERIFICATION:** (To be completed and signed by employee.)

Name: (Print or Type) Last	First	Middle	Birth Name
Address: Street Name and Number	City	State	ZIP Code
Date of Birth (Month/Day/Year)		Social Security Number	

I attest, under penalty of perjury, that I am (check a box):

☐ 1. A citizen or national of the United States.
☐ 2. An alien lawfully admitted for permanent residence (Alien Number A _____).
☐ 3. An alien authorized by the Immigration and Naturalization Service to work in the United States (Alien Number A _____ ,
or Admission Number _____ , expiration of employment authorization, if any _____).

I attest, under penalty of perjury, the documents that I have presented as evidence of identity and employment eligibility are genuine and relate to me. I am aware that federal law provides for imprisonment and/or fine for any false statements or use of false documents in connection with this certificate.

Signature	Date (Month/Day/Year)

PREPARER. TRANSLATOR CERTIFICATION (To be completed if prepared by person other than the employee). I attest, under penalty of perjury, that the above was prepared by me at the request of the named individual and is based on all information of which I have any knowledge.

Signature	Name (Print or Type)		
Address (Street Name and Number)	City	State	Zip Code

2 **EMPLOYER REVIEW AND VERIFICATION:** (To be completed and signed by employer.)

Instructions:
Examine one document from List A and check the appropriate box. **_OR_** examine one document from List B **_and_** one from List C and check the appropriate boxes.
Provide the **_Document Identification Number_** and **_Expiration Date_** for the document checked.

List A Documents that Establish Identity and Employment Eligibility	List B Documents that Establish Identity	and	List C Documents that Establish Employment Eligibility
☐ 1. United States Passport ☐ 2. Certificate of United States Citizenship ☐ 3. Certificate of Naturalization ☐ 4. Unexpired foreign passport with attached Employment Authorization ☐ 5. Alien Registration Card with photograph	☐ 1. A State-issued driver's license or a State-issued I.D. card with a photograph, or information, including name, sex, date of birth, height, weight, and color of eyes. (Specify State)_____ ☐ 2. U.S. Military Card ☐ 3. Other (Specify document and issuing authority) _____		☐ 1. Original Social Security Number Card (other than a card stating it is not valid for employment) ☐ 2. A birth certificate issued by State, county, or municipal authority bearing a seal or other certification ☐ 3. Unexpired INS Employment Authorization Specify form # _____
Document Identification # _____	**_Document Identification_** # _____		**_Document Identification_** # _____
Expiration Date (if any) _____	**_Expiration Date (if any)_** _____		**_Expiration Date (if any)_** _____

CERTIFICATION: I attest, under penalty of perjury, that I have examined the documents presented by the above individual, that they appear to be genuine and to relate to the individual named, and that the individual, to the best of my knowledge, is eligible to work in the United States.

Signature	Name (Print or Type)	Title
Employer Name	Address	Date

Form I-9 (05/07/87)
OMB No. 1115-0136

U.S. Department of Justice
Immigration and Naturalization Service

sex, union activity or membership, or for other reasons covered in later chapters.

* Provide a workplace free from recognizable hazards to the employee's safety or health.

* Make required contributions for workers' compensation, unemployment insurance, and Social Security.

* Make required deductions from the employee's pay for the worker's income tax and Social Security payments.

* Not divulge to other persons any confidential or medical information in the employee's personnel file.

* Comply with federal, state, and local laws covering other aspects of employment.

* Comply with the terms of any employment contract with the employee or with any agreement with a union representing the worker.

The enforcement of an employer's duty to an employee varies according to the nature of the duty. Some duties may be enforced through court action, while others are enforced through action by government agencies. Later chapters cover these matters in more detail.

Independent Contractors

Not all arrangements in which one person agrees to perform services for another creates an employer-employee relationship. It largely depends on whether the person for whom the work is being performed controls the manner and means by which the work will be performed. If that person has that right, he or she becomes the employer and the worker the employee. However, if the person doing the work has the right to decide how to provide the promised work or services, he or she may be considered an independent contractor rather than an employee. Self-employed electricians, plumbers, and carpenters are examples of independent contractors when they control how they will perform the work, can hire their own employees, are answerable to the person for whom they do the work only as to the final product or result, and get their pay (or profit) on the basis of the difference between their contract price and the cost of doing the work.

A person employing an independent contractor does not have to withhold payroll or Social Security taxes from the contractor's pay and does not have to negotiate with any union that may represent the contractor or its employees. Independent contractors are also not considered employees under federal equal employment opportunity law.

Agents

An agent is a person authorized to act on another person's behalf with a third person. An employee is generally not an employer's agent unless given that authority by the employer. On the other hand, an employer can give another person the authority to act as its agent for specific purposes without making that person an employee.

Even though an employee has not been authorized by the employer to be its agent and therefore cannot bind it in business dealings with another person, the employer can still be held responsible for an employee's actions when the employee injures a third person during the course of employment, regardless of whether the employer actually authorized the employee's misdeed. An employer, however, is generally not liable if the employee inflicts the injury while acting outside the scope of employment.

Whether an injury was inflicted in "the scope of employment" is often a difficult question requiring the advice of competent legal counsel in specific cases. The same can also be true in determining whether workers are employees or independent contractors.

4

TERMINATING THE EMPLOYMENT RELATIONSHIP

Most employment relationships are entered into for an indefinite period of time and can be terminated by the worker at any time for any reason by simply quitting. An employer can likewise terminate an indefinite employment relationship by discharging the employee at any time, for any reason, or, for that matter, no reason at all, provided the employer does not violate any employment contract with the employee, any union contract, or any law restricting the circumstances in which the employee can be fired.

An employment relationship that can be terminated by either the employer or the employee at any time for any reason is known as an "employment at will."

Tenure

Some jobs, such as many teaching positions, provide for job tenure after a person serves a probationary period or reaches a certain job level. A probationary worker can usually be fired at any time, but a person with tenure is considered to have permanent employment status and cannot be terminated except according to procedures that have been spelled out in advance.

Employment Contracts

An employer and an employee can enter into a written employment contract stating the terms of their agreement, including the length of time the employment will last. When the contract states that the job is for a definite period of time, the employer cannot terminate the worker before that time is up unless it has valid grounds for firing the employee. But if there is no contract, or the contract is silent on the job's duration, the relationship is considered an employment at will.

An employee, on the other hand, can stop working for an employer at any time, even though he or she has signed a contract stating the length of time the job will last. Courts will not ordinarily force employees to continue in the service of an employer for whom they no longer want to work. However, an employee's right to work

15

for another employer may be restricted if the employee has agreed in writing to perform services only for the employer he or she is quitting and not for a competitor. Courts will generally hold employees to that aspect of the contract by barring them from working for a competitor, provided the restriction is reasonable, is not for too long a period of time, and does not prevent them from earning a living in another line of work that is not in competition with the prior employer.

An employment contract between an employer and an employee, or a collective bargaining agreement between an employer and a union representing its workers, can state the circumstances in which an employee can be fired, although the length of the employment remains indefinite. Under a union contract, for example, a worker's job is not usually guaranteed for any set period of time even though the contract itself may run for two or three years, but the worker cannot be discharged unless the employer has good or just cause.

PERMANENT REPLACEMENTS

In some circumstances an employer cannot discharge an employee, but can "permanently replace" the employee with a new worker. Unlike a discharge, this action does not terminate the employment relationship between the employer and employee.

This situation occurs when employees strike to gain better pay or benefits (which is referred to as an "economic" strike). Despite a strike, an employer has the right to continue operating its business. The law, attempting to balance these respective rights of employers and employees, prohibits an employer from firing the striking workers, but allows it to hire new employees to replace those on strike.

If the strike is settled or abandoned, the employer must allow striking employees to return to their jobs unless the employer has hired new employees as permanent replacements to fill the jobs held by the strikers. Although the replacements do not have to be discharged to make room for the returning strikers, the employer must place on a preferential hiring list any striker whose job was filled by a replacement and offer him or her a job when one opens up.

Many strike settlements, however, include a commitment by the employer to the union representing the striking workers to promptly restore the strikers to their jobs and, if necessary, discharge the replacements to make room for the returning strikers. But in doing so the employer may be liable to the terminated replacements for breach of its employment agreement with them if it had indicated to them that they were being given permanent employment.

Interference With an Employment Contract

An employer may offer an employee of another employer a job, but it cannot interfere with a lawful employment relationship by maliciously enticing an employee to quit a job, nor can it, or anyone else, maliciously cause the employee's discharge. Such conduct is called "tortious" interference with an employment contract. Injured employees or employers, as the case may be, can sue the wrongdoer for the injury it causes by such unlawful interference.

Termination Notice and Severance Pay

In the absence of a contract or other agreement, neither an employer nor an employee has to give advance notice before terminating the employment relationship, and an employer does not have to provide severance pay to terminated workers. However, all states require that terminated workers be paid the wages they have earned at the time of discharge or by the next regular pay day.

Terminations Caused by Plant Closings

A number of states have adopted measures dealing with employee terminations caused by the closing of a plant or facility.

In Wisconsin an employer planning to close a plant must notify the state's labor department in advance and, in Maryland, state employees must be given six months' notice when the facility where they work is to be closed.

In Maine an employer must give its employees advance notice of a plant closing, and if the plant is moved and relocated more than 100 miles from the old location, the employer must provide severance pay to its workers. If the business has no assets, the employees may receive unpaid wages for up to two weeks from a special state fund.

Plant closing legislative measures adopted in 11 other states (Alabama, California, Hawaii, Illinois, Maryland, Massachusetts, Michigan, New York, Pennsylvania, Washington, and Wisconsin) provide for programs ranging from the encouragement of voluntary cooperation between the business being closed and the state labor department to alleviate the impact of the closing on the affected employees, to programs that provide technical and financial assistance to the affected workers to permit them to assume the ownership and operation of the business being closed.

Terminations Resulting From Bankruptcy

Workers losing their jobs because their employer's business becomes bankrupt can file a claim with the bankruptcy court for unpaid wages. If they earn wages for work during the 90-day period prior to the time the employer files for bankruptcy or during the 90-day period prior to the termination of the business, the employees become priority creditors and are entitled to full payment, up to $2,000, for the wages they earned during these periods.

Continuation of Medical Insurance

Employers in Connecticut, Iowa, Maine, and Ohio must allow laid-off or terminated employees to continue to receive any existing health insurance for a period ranging from 90 days to six months. Recent federal legislation requires employers with 20 or more workers to extend existing health insurance coverage for up to 18 months to employees who leave work for any reason and to those whose work hours are reduced.

Legal Restrictions on "At Will" Terminations

Various federal and state laws, noted below, restrict the circumstances in which an employer can terminate its workers. An increasing number of state courts have also held that there are circumstances, in addition to those spelled out in statutes, in which an employer's right to discharge employees "at will" may be restricted.

In some cases courts have ruled that an employee handbook is something like an employment contract and that it can be relied upon by a discharged worker as a basis for challenging the employer's grounds for firing the employee. Courts in other cases have held that an employee cannot be terminated for refusing to perform an unlawful act on the ground that a discharge in this circumstance would be against "public policy."

In most of the "at will" cases in which courts have held that an employer cannot fire a worker, the employer had attempted to discharge an employee for exercising the right to file a claim for workers' compensation.

An employee's discharge that can be challenged through direct court action is often referred to as a "wrongful" or "abusive" discharge to distinguish it from an ."unlawful" discharge, which is one prohibited by a statute. A challenge to an alleged unlawful discharge is generally made to a government agency before going to court.

Federal Statutory Limitations on Terminating Workers

Federal laws, particularly legislation enacted in recent years, have placed far greater restrictions on an employer's right to terminate its workers than the courts have.

The two most well-known of the laws restricting an employer's right to discharge workers are the National Labor Relations Act (NLRA) and Title VII of the 1964 Civil Rights Act, both of which are discussed in more detail in later chapters. Briefly, the NLRA prohibits employers from discharging employees for union activity, lack of union activity, protected concerted activity, or for filing charges or giving testimony under the NLRA.

Title VII prohibits terminations based on a person's race, color, religion, sex, or national origin or in reprisal for exercising Title VII rights.

The NLRA and Title VII, however, are not the only federal laws restricting an employer's right to fire workers. Other federal laws containing prohibitions on discharges are:

- *Age Discrimination in Employment Act*—prohibits discharge of workers 40 years of age or older because of their age.

- *Rehabilitation Act*—prohibits federal contractors from discriminating against handicapped workers.

- *Fair Labor Standards Act*—prohibits discharge of workers for exercising rights guaranteed by the minimum wage and overtime provisions of the Act.

- *Occupational Safety and Health Act*—prohibits discharge of workers in reprisal for exercising rights under the Act.

- *Vietnam Era Veterans' Readjustment Assistance Act*—prohibits discharge of returning veterans for a limited period of time.

- *Employee Retirement Income Security Act*—prohibits discharge of workers to prevent employees from receiving vested pension benefits.

- *Energy Reorganization Act*—prohibits discharge of employees who participate in any proceeding under the Act.

- *Railroad Safety Act*—prohibits discharge of employees who institute or testify in any proceeding relating to the enforcement of railroad safety laws, or who refuse to work because of work conditions reasonably believed to be dangerous.

- *Federal Water Pollution Control Act*—prohibits discharge of employees who institute or participate in any proceeding under the Act.

- *Judiciary and Judicial Procedure Act*—prohibits discharge of workers for serving on a jury.

- *Consumer Credit Protection Act*—prohibits discharge of employees for wage garnishment for one indebtedness.

- *Bankruptcy Act*—prohibits discharge of employees who file for bankruptcy.

- *Immigration Reform and Control Act*—prohibits discharge of employees because of national origin or citizenship status.

- *Child Support Enforcement Act*—prohibits discharge of employees whose wages are withheld for child support.

- *Surface Transportation Assistance Act*—prohibits discharge of employees who file complaints relating to commercial vehicle safety.

State Laws Restricting the Discharge of Workers

Many states, as well as the federal government, have enacted laws restricting the circumstances in which workers can be terminated. Some states have adopted the same restrictions as the federal government, while others have extended the scope of the restrictions. Many states, for example, prohibit discharge for such matters as political activity, sexual preference, military duty, refusing to take a lie detector test, exercising a government-protected right, testifying at a court hearing, or having an arrest or conviction record. And, in 1987, Montana became the first state to enact an "at will" law that prohibits an employer from firing an employee without good cause.

Whistleblowers. A growing number of states (currently 21) have adopted legislation prohibiting employers from terminating "whistleblowers," employees who report unlawful activity by their employer. Most of these laws apply to public employees, but the laws in California, Hawaii, Maine, Michigan, Minnesota, New Hampshire, New Jersey, New York, North Carolina, and Oregon also extend to private employees.

The issue in most discharge cases, whether before a court or administrative agency, relates to whether a worker was fired because of race, sex, or union activity. There is further discussion on these matters later in the book.

5
PRIVACY IN THE WORKPLACE

The right to privacy is the right to be free from unwarranted intrusion by others. Some courts call it the "right to be left alone."

This right is significantly limited for both employers and employees, but in different ways. An employer's privacy is affected when, among other things, it must file various reports and forms with the government relating to information about its business and employees. Employers are also subject to investigation by government agencies to determine their compliance with workplace laws and regulations.

An employee's privacy is largely affected by an employer's right to obtain information about the people it hires. This need for information is considered reasonable when it relates to the employer's interest in knowing about an employee's competence, reliability, and honesty as a worker, or when required by the government to obtain information about a worker.

A trucking company subject to regulation by the federal Interstate Commerce Commission, for example, is required by federal regulation to check the prior three-year employment history of a person it is considering hiring as a driver. A company holding a government defense contract must have a security check run on an employee who will have access to classified national defense information.

In some circumstances an employer's potential legal liability may require it to investigate a worker's background. This can arise when an employer hires a worker for a job allowing access to a person's living quarters, such as a job as a furniture mover or as a maintenance worker in an apartment building. The employer can be held liable if the worker criminally assaults or injures a person in his or her home or apartment when the employer failed to check the employee's background and a check would have revealed that the employee had a criminal record or showed other signs of a tendency toward violence.

More than half the states have also enacted laws requiring background investigations to determine whether persons who operate or are employed by a child care facility have a criminal history of sex offenses or child abuse.

Government and Union Intrusions on Employee Privacy

There can also be intrusions on a worker's privacy by the government and, to a lesser extent, by unions.

If the worker is union "represented," for example, the union has the right to know such things as the worker's home address, job, and pay, and pursuant to a union shop contract, can require the worker to pay union dues and fees as a condition of keeping his or her job.

The government for its part investigates and fingerprints persons applying for federal jobs and, as noted before, requires private employers to investigate their employees' background in some circumstances. It also requires, as discussed in later chapters, that employers report on the race, nationality, and sex of their workers, and that individual employees submit to the desire of the majority in deciding whether to have an agent represent them in negotiating their wages and working conditions with their employer. The government requires workers to pay income and Social Security taxes and has the right to investigate workers' compliance with the tax laws. Further, the government can request that workers undergo medical tests to determine the level of toxic substances where they work, or to determine whether they use unlawful substances.

Limitations on the Intrusions on an Employee's Privacy

Just as there are limitations on an employee's right to privacy, there are also limitations on the intrusion on that right by employers, unions, and government.

- An employer can contact a worker's previous employers for information about the individual's work history and can contact references that he or she provides. However, if the employer intends to ask for an investigative report about the person from a consumer reporting agency, the federal Fair Credit Reporting Act requires the employer to notify the individual and provide a copy of the report if the individual requests one. This law also prohibits a creditor from calling an employee at work or from contacting the employer about the debt without the worker's consent.

- Under the federal Crime Control and Safe Streets Act an employer cannot intercept an employee's confidential communication. In Virginia an employer cannot listen in on an employee's phone call with a customer without first informing the employee that such phone conversations may be monitored.

- An employer may provide information about a former employee to another employer who is considering hiring the former employee, as long as the information is not false or derogatory. If it is, the employer may be liable to the employee for defamation of character. An employer in some circumstances may be sued for intrusions on the employee's privacy if the employer makes public disclosure of embarrassing private information about the employee, such as revealing medical information or intelligence test scores found in the employee's personnel file.

- In Oregon and Washington an employer that examines a job applicant's criminal record must advise the applicant of such action. In Massachusetts an ex-offender receiving a pardon from the governor does not have to state on a job application that he or she had been convicted, and in Rhode Island an ex-offender whose criminal record has been expunged may state that he or she has never been convicted.

- An employer may search an employee's clothing or possessions for the theft of company property. However, if the circumstances of the employee's detention are unreasonable, the employer may be liable for false imprisonment.

- An employer can require that employees take a medical examination or be tested for drugs to determine their fitness to perform the required work. However, in Massachusetts and Wisconsin employers cannot test employees for AIDS (Acquired Immune Deficiency Syndrome). More than half the states also have laws providing that if an employee is required to take a medical examination, the employer must pay for it. In all states medical information must be kept confidential.

- Employees can be required to take a lie detector test except in those states where such tests are not allowed without the worker's consent. The following states and the District of Columbia restrict the use of lie detectors: Alaska, California, Connecticut, Delaware, Georgia, Hawaii, Idaho, Iowa, Maine, Maryland, Massachusetts, Michigan, Minnesota, Missouri, Montana, Nebraska, Nevada, New Jersey, New York, Oregon, Pennsylvania, Rhode Island, Tennessee, Utah, Vermont, Washington, West Virginia, and Wisconsin. In Washington a manufacturer or distributor of controlled substances is exempt from that state's general prohibition on the use of lie detectors.

- Workers in California, Connecticut, Delaware, Idaho, Illinois, Massachusetts, Michigan, New Hampshire, New York, Pennsylvania, Rhode Island, Washington, and Wisconsin have the right to see their personnel files. Public employees in Alaska and Maine also have the right to see their personnel files.

- Unions generally have the right to request information about the workers they represent for purposes of negotiating wages and working conditions. Some information, however, is restricted. An employer, for instance, is not required to turn over to a union a worker's test score without the worker's consent.

- The National Labor Relations Act allows that a union, with the employer's agreement, can have a contract requiring that workers become union members as a condition of employment. Courts, however, have interpreted this provision to mean that employees are not actually required to join a union but must pay union dues and fees. Workers who are union members have the right to resign their memberships at any time except for reasonable restrictions on the timing of a resignation contained in a union contract or constitution. However, under Section 14(b) of the Act, 21 states presently have right-to-work laws that prohibit employers and unions from entering into agreements requiring that workers join unions or pay dues as a condition of employment. These states are Alabama, Arizona, Arkansas, Florida, Georgia, Idaho, Iowa, Kansas, Louisiana, Mississippi, Nebraska, Nevada, North Carolina, North Dakota, South Carolina, South Dakota, Tennessee, Texas, Utah, Virginia, and Wyoming.

- The government's intrusions on an employer's or employee's right to privacy are generally restricted by the U.S. Constitution, which prohibits the government from engaging in an unreasonable search or seizure of a person or requiring a person to incriminate himself or herself. An employer in some circumstances can therefore require that a government agency wanting to inspect its facility obtain a search warrant. Federal privacy legislation allows workers to have access to information about them contained in the files of government agencies and restricts the disclosure of such information to unauthorized persons.

6
WAGES AND
WORKING CONDITIONS

An employee can agree to work for an employer for the wages and under the working conditions the employer offers or according to those on which they mutually agree, provided the arrangement does not violate any law or any contract the employer has with a union that determines the employee's pay rate. If the employee's wage or salary is not specified, it is determined according to the wage paid in the area for the type of work the employee performs.

A worker's pay can be based on salary, work performed by the hour, or piecework. Most states require that, however the employee's pay is determined, it be paid at regular intervals, usually at least every two weeks, in cash or negotiable check. About half the states require that employers notify employees in writing of their wage rates, with some requiring that employees be given a statement containing an itemization of hours worked, wages paid, and deductions made. Missouri, Pennsylvania, South Carolina, and Texas also require that workers be notified in advance of any change in their rate of pay. Connecticut and Virginia require employers to notify their employees in advance of any plan to terminate existing health insurance. In most states a worker can request assistance from the state's labor department to collect unpaid wages.

Minimum Wage

The wage law with which most employers must comply is the federal Fair Labor Standards Act (FLSA), which is also referred to as the minimum wage or wage-hour law. The FLSA, covered in the next chapter, sets the national minimum wage that employees covered by law must receive whether paid by the hour or by salary. Most states also have their own minimum wage laws, and when an employer is covered by both federal and state laws, it must pay the higher of the two.

Hours of Work

The FLSA does not restrict the number of hours an employee over 18 years old can be required to work in a day or a week, but it does require that workers be paid at the rate of 1½ times their regular hourly rate for hours worked in excess of 40 hours in a workweek. Some states require daily overtime pay.

Every state except Delaware, Hawaii, Michigan, New Jersey, and Tennessee have laws containing some form of restriction on the maximum number of hours employees can be required to work, such as placing a limit on the hours that can be worked in a week, requiring a 24-hour rest period each week, or prohibiting work on Sundays. For safety reasons, federal transportation laws restrict the number of hours a truck driver, bus driver, or airline pilot subject to federal regulation can work in a day or week. About half the states require that employers allow workers time off for breaks or meals after working a specified number of hours.

Fringe Benefits

A fringe benefit is any benefit a worker receives in addition to pay, such as paid holidays, vacations, sick leave, medical insurance, and pensions. Although most employers provide some fringe benefits to their workers, federal and state laws do not require the payment of fringe benefits except for the payments that have to be made on the employees' behalf for Social Security, workers' compensation, and unemployment insurance, or when an employer is performing work under a government contract. However, all states require employers that do provide health insurance to their employees to provide minimum benefits, usually by requiring coverage for newborn children and for pregnancy.

Working Conditions

The law that directly affects the conditions under which workers are permitted to work is the federal Occupational Safety and Health Act (OSHA), which requires employers to provide working conditions that are free from recognizable hazards to the workers' safety and health.

The federal Equal Employment Opportunity Commission affects working conditions indirectly by requiring that, whatever the working conditions are, they be provided to workers on a nondiscriminatory basis. The federal National Labor Relations Act does not prescribe working conditions, but does allow workers to select a union to negotiate on their behalf concerning their working conditions as well as their pay and benefits.

Smoking in the Workplace

In a trend that started in the last two years, a growing number of states have enacted laws requiring employers to develop rules regulating smoking in the workplace, usually by requiring employers to designate smoking and non-smoking areas. States that currently have such laws are Arizona, Connecticut, Maine, New Hampshire, New Jersey, Rhode Island, Utah, and Vermont.

Payroll Deductions

Employers by law must withhold income and Social Security taxes from an employee's pay. In the absence of a law, they may also make deductions from a worker's pay for cash shortages or other expenses caused or incurred by the employee, and, with the employee's consent, make deductions for union dues. However, about two-thirds of the states have laws placing restrictions on the deductions an employer can make from an employee's pay without his or her consent. The FLSA also prohibits deductions if they reduce the worker's pay below the federal minimum wage.

A 1984 federal law, the Child Support Enforcement Act, directs the states to enact laws requiring employers to withhold from their employees' wages any amount determined to be due under a child support order issued by a court or administrative agency. Employers failing to comply with such a law are to be subject to a fine.

Time Off From Work

An employer does not have to give employees time off from work except when required by law or by union contract. Employers also do not have to give employees time off on government-declared "legal" holidays. Most states, however, do require that employees be allowed time off to vote, perform jury duty, or serve on temporary military duty. Some states also require that employers grant time off under other specified circumstances.

Minnesota, for instance, requires employers to grant leave to employees attending political meetings or conventions. Indiana in effect requires that employees engaged in fire fighting be allowed time off by prohibiting their discharge for being absent because of such activity. The states of Maryland, New York, South Carolina, and West Virginia similarly prohibit the discharge of employees who are required to be away from work to participate in certain court or administrative proceedings.

Federal law in effect requires that time off be allowed for workers who enlist or are drafted by requiring that they be allowed to return to their old jobs when they complete their active military duty.

Unless required by law or union contract, an employer does not have to pay employees for the time they take off from work.

Maternity Leave

Nine states (California, Connecticut, Hawaii, Illinois, Massachusetts, Montana, New Hampshire, Ohio, and Washington) require that pregnant employees be allowed unpaid leave, and federal law requires employers that allow time off to employees for illness or for other medical reasons to allow time off to women because of pregnancy.

Mechanic's Lien

A mechanic's lien is a means by which a worker can enforce a claim for payment for work that he or she performs for another person and usually arises when the worker has possession of the property on which the work was performed. The worker has the right to retain possession of the property until the work is paid for and, by following the legal procedures required by state law for enforcing a lien, can sell the property to satisfy the claim for payment. A contractor or laborer can also obtain a lien on a building on which work was performed.

Garnishments and Wage Assignments

A garnishment is a legal procedure that a creditor can use to make an employee pay off a debt. In a wage garnishment proceeding, the employer is directed by a court to pay the employee's wages to the creditor until the debt is paid.

A wage assignment differs from a garnishment in that it is a voluntary agreement by the employee to transfer (assign) part of his or her wages to another person or organization to pay off a debt or for any other purpose.

All states regulate wage garnishments by limiting the amount of an employee's wages that can be garnished. Some states prohibit an employee's discharge for garnishments. These laws also provide that an employee's wages can be garnished for spousal or child support and that more of an employee's wages can be garnished for this purpose than for other forms of indebtedness.

A federal wage garnishment law, like the state laws, exempts a certain percentage of an employee's pay from a garnishment. The federal exemption is 75 percent of the worker's disposable weekly earnings, or 30 times the federal minimum wage, whichever is less. Federal law also prohibits an employer from discharging an employee for a garnishment arising from one indebtedness. The Equal Employment Opportunity Commission, moreover, considers the discharge of a minority employee for more than one garnishment to be a form of racial discrimination and is therefore prohibited.

Most states also regulate wage assignments, with some declaring that a wage assignment is not valid if its purpose is to have a worker pay off a debt.

The following pages contain a summary of state law provisions on minimum wage and working conditions. More information about these and other state laws regulating working conditions can be obtained from a state labor department. Appendix A lists the addresses of these departments.

A summary of state and federal employment laws is also included in *The BNA Policy and Practice Series.* Address inquiries to:

The Bureau of National Affairs Inc.
Attn: Customer Service
1231 25th Street, N.W.
Washington, D.C. 20037

SELECTED STATE LAW PROVISIONS CONCERNING MINIMUM WAGE AND WORKING CONDITIONS

	Minimum wage	Garnish-ments restricted	Wage assignments restricted	Deductions from wages restricted	State assistance in collecting unpaid wages	Workers not required to pay cost of medical exam	Time off to vote	Time off for jury duty	Meal and/or rest period required
Alabama		✓	✓		✓		✓	✓	
Alaska	3.85	✓	✓		✓		✓	✓	
Arizona	3.15	✓	✓	✓	✓		✓	✓	✓
Arkansas	3.35	✓	✓	✓	✓	✓	✓	✓	
California	3.35	✓	✓	✓	✓	✓	✓		✓
Colorado	3.00	✓	✓	✓	✓				
Connecticut	3.37	✓	✓	✓	✓			✓	
Delaware	3.00	✓	✓	✓	✓			✓	
District of Columbia	3.35-4.75	✓	✓	✓	✓			✓	
Florida		✓					✓		
Georgia	3.25	✓	✓		✓	✓	✓		
Hawaii	3.35	✓		✓	✓			✓	
Idaho	2.30	✓	✓	✓	✓	✓	✓	✓	✓
Illinois	3.35	✓	✓	✓	✓		✓	✓	
Indiana	2.00	✓	✓	✓	✓		✓	✓	
Iowa	1.60	✓	✓	✓	✓		✓	✓	
Kansas	1.60	✓	✓	✓		✓	✓	✓	
Kentucky	3.35	✓	✓	✓		✓		✓	✓
Louisiana		✓	✓	✓		✓			
Maine	3.35	✓	✓	✓	✓				

State	Rate								
Maryland	3.35	✓	✓					✓	
Massachusetts	3.55	✓	✓	✓	✓	✓	✓	✓	✓
Michigan	3.35	✓	✓	✓	✓	✓		✓	✓
Minnesota	3.35	✓	✓	✓			✓	✓	
Mississippi									
Missouri		✓		✓			✓	✓	
Montana	3.35	✓	✓	✓	✓	✓	✓	✓	✓
Nebraska	1.60	✓	✓	✓	✓	✓		✓	✓
Nevada	2.75	✓	✓	✓	✓				✓
New Hampshire	3.45	✓	✓	✓	✓	✓	✓		
New Jersey	3.35	✓	✓	✓		✓	✓		
New Mexico	3.35	✓	✓	✓					
New York	3.35	✓	✓	✓	✓	✓	✓	✓	✓
North Carolina	3.35	✓	✓	✓	✓	✓	✓	✓	✓
North Dakota	2.80-3.10	✓	✓	✓	✓	✓	✓	✓	✓
Ohio	2.30	✓	✓	✓	✓	✓	✓	✓	✓
Oklahoma	3.35	✓	✓	✓	✓		✓	✓	✓
Oregon	3.35	✓	✓	✓	✓				
Pennsylvania	3.35	✓	✓	✓	✓			✓	✓
Rhode Island	3.55	✓	✓	✓	✓			✓	✓
South Carolina		✓		✓					
South Dakota	2.80	✓	✓	✓	✓	✓	✓	✓	
Tennessee		✓	✓	✓		✓	✓	✓	
Texas	1.40	✓		✓					✓
Utah	2.50-2.75	✓	✓					✓	✓
Vermont	3.45	✓	✓	✓	✓	✓		✓	
Virginia	2.65	✓	✓		✓	✓			
Washington	2.30	✓	✓	✓	✓	✓		✓	✓
West Virginia	3.35	✓	✓	✓	✓	✓	✓	✓	✓
Wisconsin	3.25	✓	✓	✓		✓	✓	✓	✓
Wyoming	1.60	✓	✓	✓	✓	✓	✓	✓	✓

7

MINIMUM WAGE

The Fair Labor Standards Act (FLSA) sets the minimum wage that employees covered by the law must receive and requires employers to pay overtime rates to employees who are required to work more than 40 hours in a workweek.

Employees Covered by the FLSA

Unless specifically exempted, all employees engaged in interstate commerce—workers, for example, who make goods that will be sent from one state into another—must be paid the minimum wage and overtime pay set by the FLSA. This also includes employees engaged in interstate communications or transportation; employees in distributing industries such as wholesaling who receive, order, or keep records of goods moving in commerce; and employees who mine, produce, process, or distribute goods for commerce, even though the goods may leave the state through another firm.

In addition to those employees who are covered because they are engaged in interstate commerce, employees of the following enterprises are also covered by the FLSA:

- Laundries and dry cleaners;
- Construction companies;
- Hospitals;
- Homes for the aged, mentally ill, or handicapped;
- Institutions of higher education;
- Retail and service establishments with sales or business of at least $365,000 a year; and
- Any other type of business with annual sales or business of not less than $250,000.

Domestic workers such as maids, day workers, housekeepers, chauffeurs, cooks, or full-time baby-sitters are covered by the FLSA if they receive at least $50 in cash wages in a calendar quarter from their employer or work a total of more than eight hours in a week for one or more employers.

Minimum Wage and Working Hours

Workers covered by the FLSA must be paid at least $3.35 an hour and must be paid for all the hours they work. This is generally considered to be all the time they are required by their employer to be at their place of work or on duty, including such activities as learning their jobs, correcting the work of others, and setting up machines. It does not ordinarily include the commuting time getting to and from a place of work.

Mealtime is not considered work time unless the employee is required to tend a machine or do other work while eating or is not allowed enough time to eat. Thirty minutes is usually considered enough time for meals.

The FLSA also does not require an employer to pay an employee for hours not worked because of holidays, vacations, illness, lack of work, or other similar reasons. The employer can, of course, pay workers for such nonwork time, and a union contract can require an employer to pay more than is required by the FLSA.

Gratuities

If an employee customarily and regularly receives more than $30 a month in tips, his or her employer may credit the tips toward the employee's wages. This tip credit, however, cannot exceed 40 percent of the minimum wage.

Overtime Pay

Employees covered by the FLSA must be paid a higher hourly rate for overtime work, which for purposes of the FLSA is work in excess of 40 hours in a workweek. A "workweek" under the FLSA is a fixed and regularly recurring period of seven consecutive 24-hour periods. It does not have to coincide with a calendar week. A "workweek," provided it is a fixed period, can begin any day of the week and any hour of the day.

Overtime must be paid at a rate of 1½ times the worker's *regular* pay rate (which must be at least the minimum wage but for many workers is more) for each hour worked in excess of the 40 hours in that employee's workweek. A hospital or residential care establishment, however, may pay overtime on the basis of a 14-day work period instead of a workweek.

The FLSA does not require an employer to pay overtime rates or other "premium" pay to an employee for work on a Saturday, Sunday, or holiday, unless the hours worked on those days are in excess of the 40 hours in that employee's workweek.

Employees covered by FLSA who are paid by salary, piecework, or commission must also receive the minimum wage and overtime pay. Their hourly rate is usually determined by dividing their weekly pay by the number of hours worked. Overtime is then based on 1½ times this rate. For example, a salaried worker who is paid

$136 a week for a 40-hour workweek earns a regular hourly rate of $3.40 ($136 ÷ 40). If the employee works more than 40 hours, he or she would be entitled to $5.10 for each overtime hour ($3.40 x 1½).

FLSA Exemptions

Some employees are exempt from the minimum wage or overtime provision, or both. However, each exemption is narrowly defined under the law. An employer is therefore cautioned to carefully check the exact terms and conditions of the exemption before applying it. The following are examples of some of the exemptions.

Exemptions from both minimum wage and overtime:

- Executive, administrative, and professional employees, and outside sales personnel;
- Employees of certain individually owned and operated small retail and service establishments not part of a covered enterprise;
- Employees of certain seasonal amusement or recreational establishments;
- Employees of certain small newspapers or switchboard operators of small telephone companies; and
- Farm workers employed by anyone who used no more than 500 man-days of farm labor in a calendar quarter.

Exemptions from overtime provisions only:

- Sales persons, partsmen, and mechanics engaged primarily in selling or servicing automobiles, trucks, farm implements, or aircraft;
- Certain highly paid commission employees of retail or service establishments;
- Employees of motion picture theaters; and
- Farm workers.

Young Workers

Workers 18 years of age or older may work at any time in any job. The FLSA, however, restricts the types of work and hours of work for persons under 18 years old.

Workers 16 or 17 years old may work in any occupation except those declared hazardous by the Secretary of Labor. This hazardous work includes:

- Manufacturing or storing explosives;
- Driving a motor vehicle or being an outside helper;
- Mining;
- Logging and sawmilling;

- Being exposed to radioactive substances and ionizing radiations;
- Using power-driven hoisting apparatus;
- Using power-driven bakery machines;
- Manufacturing brick, tile, and related products; and
- Wrecking, demolition, and ship-wrecking operations.

The following are also hazardous, but exemptions under specified standards are provided for apprentices and student-learners:

- Power-driven metal forming, punching, and shearing machines;
- Power-driven woodworking machines;
- Meat packing or processing;
- Power-driven paper products machines;
- Power-driven circular saws, band saws, and guillotine shears;
- Roofing operations; and
- Excavation operations.

Workers 14 or 15 years old may work in office, clerical, and sales jobs, and in retail, food service, and gasoline service establishments performing such duties as:

- Cashiering, price marking, and tagging;
- Assembling orders, packing, shelving, bagging, and carrying out orders;
- Serving foods and beverages;
- Car washing and polishing and operating gas pumps; or
- Doing errand and delivery work by foot, bicycle, or public transportation.

However, 14- or 15-year-olds may *not* work:

- During school hours;
- Before 7 a.m. or after 7 p.m. (9 p.m. from June 1 through Labor Day);
- More than 18 hours during school weeks;
- More than three hours on school days; or
- More than 40 hours in nonschool weeks.

Workers *at any age* may:

- Deliver newspapers;
- Act or perform in motion pictures or in theatrical, radio or television productions;

- Work for their parents, except in manufacturing, mining, or hazardous nonfarm jobs; or
- Work on any farm owned or operated by their parents.

Farm Work

- Workers 16 years old may work at any time in any farm job.
- Workers 14 or 15 years old may work outside school hours in any farm job except those declared hazardous by the Secretary of Labor.
- Workers 12 or 13 years old may work outside school hours in nonhazardous farm jobs with their parents' written consent, or may work on a farm where their parents are employed.
- Persons younger than 12 years old may work outside school hours in nonhazardous farm jobs with their parents' written consent on farms where the employees do not have to be paid the minimum wage.
- Minors 10 or 11 years old may work for no more than 8 weeks between June 1 and October 15 for employers who receive approval from the Secretary of Labor. This work must be confined to hand-harvested short season crops outside school hours under very limited and specified circumstances prescribed by the Secretary of Labor .

Young workers must be paid the minimum wage and overtime pay rates regardless of their age, unless the Wage-Hour Administrator has expressly certified that they may be paid a lower wage.

Recordkeeping

The wage and hour records required to be kept by employers do not have to be in any particular form, but should contain the following information about employees covered by the FLSA:

- Name, home address, and birth date if under 19 years old;
- Sex and occupation;
- Hour and day when the employee's workweek begins;
- Regular hourly pay for any week when overtime is worked;
- Total daily or weekly straight time earnings;
- Total overtime pay for the workweek;
- Deductions or additions to wages;
- Total wages paid each pay period; and
- Date of payment and pay period covered.

Subminimum Wages

Learners and apprentices under certain circumstances may be paid less than the minimum wage, as may full-time students in retail or service establishments, agriculture, or institutions of higher learning. Workers who are 65 or older or mentally or physically disabled and whose earning abilities are reduced may also be employed below the minimum wage. However, before employers can pay less than the minimum wage, they must obtain a special certificate from the U.S. Labor Department's Wage and Hour Administrator.

What the FLSA Does Not Require

Although federal or state laws or a union contract may require the following, the FLSA does not require an employer to:

* Give employees a discharge notice or a reason for discharge. (An employer, however, cannot fire or discriminate against an employee for filing a complaint involving the FLSA.)
* Provide rest periods, holidays, or vacations.
* Grant pay raises or fringe benefits.
* Set a limit on the hours of work for employees 16 years of age or older.
* Provide severance or sick pay.
* Pay premium or overtime wages for work on weekends or holidays.

FLSA Enforcement

The FLSA is enforced by compliance officers from the U.S. Department of Labor's Wage and Hour Division. These officers have the authority to conduct investigations and gather data on wages, hours of work, and other employment conditions or practices to determine whether an employer is complying with the law. Where violations are found, they may also recommend changes in employment practices in order to obtain compliance with the law.

Recovering Back Wages

Employees may recover minimum wages and/or overtime pay through one of the following procedures:

* The Wage and Hour Division may supervise the payment of back wages that the employer agrees to pay.
* The Secretary of Labor may bring a court suit for back wages.
* Employees may file a private suit for back pay. However, they may not sue if they have been paid back wages under the supervision of the Wage and Hour Division, or if the Secretary of Labor has already filed suit.

A two-year statute of limitations applies to the recovery of back pay, except that in the case of a willful violation, a three-year statute applies.

Other Federal Wage Laws

In addition to the FLSA, there are four other federal wage-hour laws that apply to employers that work under a contract with the federal government. These laws are:

- The *Walsh-Healey Act*, which requires employers furnishing materials, supplies, articles, or equipment to the government under contracts exceeding $10,000 to pay their employees the prevailing wage in the industry.

- The *Davis-Bacon Act*, which requires employers working under a government contract exceeding $2,000 involving the construction, alteration, or repair of public buildings or public works, including painting or decorating, to pay their laborers and mechanics the prevailing wages in the locality where the work is to be performed.

- The *McNamara-O'Hara Service Contract Act*, which requires employers furnishing services (e.g., guards and watchmen) to the government under contracts exceeding $2,500 to pay their employees the prevailing wages and fringe benefits in the locality.

- The *Work Hours Act*, which requires the payment of overtime pay for hours worked in excess of eight per day and 40 per week to mechanics and laborers employed on any public work.

Like the FLSA, these laws are also enforced by the Wage and Hour Division of the Labor Department.

More information on the FLSA and other laws administered by the Wage and Hour Division, including the federal wage garnishment law, may be obtained from any of its local offices. They are listed in the telephone directory under the U.S. Government, Department of Labor, Employment Standards Administration, Wage and Hour Division. Its national office address is:

U.S. Department of Labor
Employment Standards Administration
Wage and Hour Division
Washington, D.C. 20210

8
JOB SAFETY

Employers are required by the federal Occupational Safety and Health Act and by many state laws to maintain a workplace free from recognized hazards to the health and safety of their employees. Twenty-five states also have what are referred to as "right-to-know" laws that require, depending on the state law, varying degrees of disclosure of information to their employees about the hazardous chemical substances they handle. States with right-to-know laws are Alabama, Alaska, California, Connecticut, Delaware, Florida, Illinois, Iowa, Louisiana, Maine, Massachusetts, Maryland, Michigan, Minnesota, Montana, New Hampshire, New Jersey, New York, North Carolina, Oregon, Pennsylvania, Rhode Island, Virginia, Washington, and West Virginia.

Occupational Safety and Health Administration

The federal safety and health act requires all businesses, except those such as mining which are subject to safety laws specifically applicable to them, to provide their workers with safe and healthful working conditions by maintaining a place of employment free from hazards that may cause serious physical harm or death. An employer is also expected to take the initiative in identifying and eliminating sources of injury to its workers. The federal law is enforced by the Labor Department's Occupational Safety and Health Administration (OSHA).

Safety Standards

In addition to eliminating recognizable hazards, employers must also comply with specific OSHA-prescribed job safety and health standards. These standards cover such matters as fire protection, construction and maintenance of equipment, worker training, machine guarding, and protective equipment to be worn by workers. Employers are further required to familiarize themselves with and to observe the OSHA standards applicable to their type of business and to inform their workers of these standards.

Employers engaged in hazardous work operations must take special care in monitoring waste sites and providing their workers with medical exams, training, and appropriate safety equipment in handling hazardous wastes.

Employee Rights

Workers have the right to report unsafe or unhealthful working conditions to OSHA. A worker in imminent danger of a job safety or health hazard can ask an employer to correct the matter or the worker can contact the nearest OSHA area office. If OSHA determines that a hazard exists, it requests the employer to eliminate the hazard and it can seek an order from a court requiring the employer to take corrective action.

An employer cannot punish or discriminate against workers for exercising their job safety and health rights by complaining about hazards to their employer, union, OSHA, or other government agencies. Workers also have the right to participate in OSHA inspections, conferences, hearings, or other OSHA-related activities.

A worker punished for exercising these rights has 30 days to complain to an OSHA area office. If after an investigation OSHA finds that the worker has been unlawfully punished it will ask the employer to reinstate the worker (if the employee was fired) and to restore any earnings or benefits the employee may have lost. If necessary, OSHA can ask a federal court to enforce its order.

In some instances, the refusal of workers to perform dangerous work may be protected by the National Labor Relations Board, usually when the worker's action was with, or on behalf of, other workers.

Variances

An employer unable to comply with an OSHA safety standard may ask OSHA for a permanent or temporary "variance" from that particular standard. A permanent variance may be granted if the employer can show that its safety practice or procedure, while not in literal compliance with OSHA's standard, is nevertheless as safe.

An employer seeking a temporary variance must establish (1) that it is unable to comply with the standard by its effective date because of the unavailability of the means to comply by that date; (2) that it is doing all it can to protect its workers against the hazard covered by the standard; (3) that it has a plan to come into compliance with the standard as soon as practicable; and (4) that it has notified its employees of its application for the variance. Its notice to the employees must inform them that they have the right to a hearing on its application.

Recordkeeping

An employer with 10 or more workers must maintain records of occupational injuries (other than those involving only first aid) and illnesses. Workers, or their representatives, have the right to review these records.

Inspections

As with many regulatory agencies, OSHA has compliance officers who have the authority to inspect business operations for violations of the law and OSHA standards. Employers can voluntarily agree to an inspection or can require that the inspector obtain a search warrant.

When an inspection is made, it ordinarily begins with a meeting ("opening conference") to discuss procedures for the inspection. The inspector then conducts a "walkaround" inspection of the facility, accompanied by representatives for the employer and its employees. The employer, of course, selects its representative. It cannot, however, select one for the employees. Their representative must be selected by the workers or their union (if they have one), or by the inspector. The employees' representative must be paid for the time spent on the inspection.

Workers have the right to talk to the inspector concerning the facility's health and safety problems and may do so on a private and confidential basis. If health hazards are found, another inspector trained as an industrial hygienist may be called in to measure levels of dust, noise, fumes, or other hazards. Test results are given to the employer's and the employees' representatives.

When the inspection is completed the inspector confers with the representatives in a closing conference concerning the conditions and practices, if any, which he or she believes constitute hazardous conditions that must be modified or eliminated ("abated") and the length of time it will take to correct them.

The inspector then files a report with OSHA's area director, who decides what citations for safety violations, if any, will be issued, the deadlines for correcting job hazards, and the penalties to be imposed.

Citations

The director may, of course, find that there were no safety violations. Should he or she find that there were violations, a written citation describing the nature of each violation and the time allowed for correcting it will be sent to the employer. The employer must post a copy of the citation at or near the place where the violation occurred for a period of three days or until the condition is corrected, whichever is longer.

Penalties

The penalty for a safety violation depends on its seriousness.

- For a willful or repeated violation the penalty may be up to $10,000—or up to six months in prison if the violation resulted in a worker's death.

- For a serious violation—one from which serious physical harm or death could result—there is a mandatory penalty of up to $1,000.

- For a nonserious violation—one that has a direct relationship to job safety but which probably would not cause serious physical harm or death—there may be a penalty of up to $1,000.

For both serious and nonserious violations, the amount of the proposed penalty the OSHA director decides to assess against the employer depends on the gravity of the hazard, the company's history of previous violations, its good-faith efforts to comply with the law, and the size of the business. Additional penalties may be assessed if an OSHA follow-up inspection shows a failure to take necessary corrective action, unless the employer can show a good-faith effort to comply.

Appeals

A citation, proposed penalty, and/or abatement date can be appealed by the employer by notifying the area director in writing within 15 days. If notice is not given within this time, the director's determination becomes final and must be complied with.

If the employer appeals (called a "notice of contest"), it must post a notice in its facility where it can be seen by its employees and inform their union (if they have one). The workers or their representative may participate in the appeal process by notifying OSHA.

Whether or not the employer appeals, the workers or their representative can challenge the time allowed by OSHA for correcting a hazard by following the same appeal procedure allowed their employer.

Administrative Hearing

After the appeal is filed, the Labor Department issues a "complaint" setting forth its position on the issues raised in the employer's appeal. The complaint must be answered by the employer within 15 days by admitting, denying, or offering to explain the allegations in the complaint.

A hearing is held sometime later before an OSHA administrative law judge. At the hearing the Labor Department has the burden of proving the issues being contested. Employers have the right to present opposing evidence and arguments in support of their position. Their employees or their representative also have the same right to participate in the hearing.

After the judge issues a decision, any party objecting to it can ask the Occupational Safety and Health Review Commission to review the judge's decision. The Review Commission, however, does not have to agree to review the case. If it does not agree, the judge's decision becomes final in 30 days. Any party adversely affected by the result can appeal to a federal appeals court.

State Enforcement

A state can take over the enforcement of job safety in its state if it can show to OSHA's satisfaction that it has an effective program. Some of the areas of the state's proposed program that OSHA will check before giving its approval include:

- *Worker rights.* The state must provide workers with the same rights that OSHA provides.

- *Standards.* The state's safety and health standards cannot provide workers with less protection than that provided by OSHA's standards.

- *Inspectors.* The state must have trained inspectors who will be effective in finding and correcting hazards.

- *Appeals.* Workers must be allowed to participate in cases involving employer appeals of penalties or deadlines for correcting hazards, and to appeal state actions relating to safety and health.

More information about OSHA can be obtained from one of its regional or area offices listed in the phone directory or by writing to:

U.S. Department of Labor
Occupational Safety and Health Administration
Washington, D.C. 20210

9
UNEMPLOYMENT BENEFITS

Unemployment insurance (also referred to as unemployment compensation) is a weekly benefit paid for a limited period of time to workers to tide them over when they are out of work through no fault of their own. Unlike workers' compensation and Social Security disability programs, which provide benefits to workers who are unable to work because of a disability, a worker applying for unemployment insurance must be able to work.

Unemployment insurance is a federal-state activity, with each state administering its own program or system. A special payroll tax on employers funds the system. However, Alabama, Alaska, and New Jersey also require employees to share a part of the cost. The amount of the employer's tax depends on the unemployment rate among its employees. An employer with a higher unemployment rate than other employers pays a higher tax. The tax is adjusted annually according to the employer's unemployment rate.

Workers Covered by Unemployment Insurance

Almost all employees performing services for which they receive compensation are covered by unemployment insurance. This includes a company's officers and executives as well as its rank-and-file workers; state and local government employees; federal workers; household workers whose employers pay them at least $1,000 (in cash) a calendar quarter; and farm workers of farm operators having payrolls of at least $20,000 in a calendar quarter or having 10 or more employees working at least part of a day each week for 20 weeks. Temporary and part-time workers are also covered, although their unemployment benefits may be less than those of full-time workers. Not covered are independent contractors, newspaper carriers under 18 years of age, certain newspaper and magazine vendors, children who work for their parents, and individuals employed by their spouses or children.

Qualifying for Benefits

A worker applying for unemployment benefits must be out of work, not at fault in causing his or her unemployment, able to work, and available for work.

Each state also requires applicants to satisfy certain work and earnings requirements to be eligible for unemployment pay. These requirements generally provide that during a "base period"—usually a recent 12-month period prior to the time the worker became unemployed—the worker must have been employed for a prescribed period of time, usually for at least two calendar quarters during the base period, or have earned a specified amount of wages during the base period, or have a combination of both.

If an unemployed worker meets his or her state's work and earnings requirements, a determination is then made of the weekly benefit amount and the duration of the payments. The amount is related to the wages earned while employed, usually 50 percent of the worker's weekly pay. Each state, however, provides for a minimum and maximum weekly payment. In 1986, for example, the minimum ranged from $10 to $62, while the maximum ranged from $95 to $310. Some states also allow additional payments for dependents.

Benefits may also be available for partial unemployment. In this case the amount is generally the difference between what the worker actually earns through partial employment and the amount of benefit he or she would have received if totally unemployed.

Duration of Benefits

The maximum length of time payments are made is 26 weeks in most states. When this time period ends, the payments end. To again be entitled to benefits, the worker must reestablish eligibility under the requirements of the state's law. Partial benefits may be received for a longer period of time in some states. Also, during times of high unemployment, a worker whose benefits are exhausted may receive payments for an extended period of time, usually for half as long as the regular period of entitlement to payments.

Able and Available

A jobless worker collecting unemployment benefits is expected to actively seek work, report for work at the local employment service office at regular intervals, and accept suitable job offers.

He or she must also be physically able to work and available for work. Workers are generally considered available for work if they are able to resume work in their customary occupation or in some other occupation reasonably consistent with their education, training, and experience. A worker may lose benefits for any week in which he or she does not look for work or is not available for work.

Disabled Workers

Workers who are unable to work because of sickness or other disability are considered in most states not to be able to work and therefore ineligible for unemployment benefits for the weeks they are unable to work. There are exceptions, however. In Colorado, employees terminated because they are physically or mentally unable to work are eligible for unemployment pay. And in North Dakota, workers who become disabled during a period of unemployment do not lose their eligibility for benefits. Five states—California, Hawaii, New Jersey, New York, and Rhode Island—also provide special disability benefits to jobless workers who are temporarily disabled because of illness or injury. In all states, disabled workers may be eligible for workers' compensation or Social Security disability benefits. Chapter 10 covers the eligibility requirements for these benefits.

Pregnancy

Benefits cannot be denied solely because of pregnancy. A pregnant woman, however, must still meet the general requirements of ability to work and availability for work despite her pregnancy.

Waiting Period

Most states require a one-week period before a person who is out of work becomes eligible for unemployment pay. There is, however, no waiting period in Alabama, Connecticut, Delaware, Iowa, Kentucky, Maine, Maryland, Michigan, Nevada, New Hampshire, or Wisconsin. In some states a worker may be compensated later for the waiting period if he or she is unemployed for a specified period of time.

Relocating

An unemployed worker moving from one locality to another—or from one state to another—continues to be entitled to unemployment benefits, provided the chances of finding a job are about the same in the new state as in the one that the worker left. If a worker moves to another state, his or her weekly benefit will be the amount that is paid in the state in which he or she became unemployed.

Disqualification

Workers who cause their own unemployment may be disqualified from some or all unemployment benefits. The grounds for disqualification vary from state to state, with the most common grounds for disqualification in all states involving situations where:

- The worker voluntarily quits a job without good reason.
- The worker gets fired for work-related misconduct.
- The worker refuses to accept suitable work without a good reason.

Most states also disqualify workers who are out of work because of a strike or other labor dispute. The laws of New York and

Rhode Island, however, provide that benefits can be paid to workers who are unemployed because of a strike or lockout after a specified waiting period.

When a worker is disqualified, it can mean that benefits will be postponed for one or more weeks (in addition to any waiting period), or that they will be denied for the duration of joblessness. The time period for disqualification depends on the reason for the disqualification and varies from state to state.

Aliens

Citizens of another country who are not lawfully admitted to the United States are not eligible for unemployment pay. However, aliens who have been lawfully admitted for permanent residence are eligible.

Claims Procedure

A claim for unemployment benefits is usually filed in person in the state employment office in the state in which the worker resides. A claims examiner determines whether the worker is eligible for benefits and, if eligible, the amount and duration of the benefits the worker will receive.

As the claim will affect the amount of unemployment tax employers will have to pay, employers are considered interested parties to the claim when one or more of their out-of-work employees files for benefits. The employer is therefore notified of the claim and allowed to state its reasons for the worker's unemployment.

If the worker disputes either the employer's reasons for his or her unemployment or the examiner's determination of eligibility, the worker has the right to a hearing and representation by an attorney or other representative. At the hearing, the worker has the right to testify and present evidence in support of the claim. Both the employee and the employer also have the right to appeal a decision by the unemployment agency to a state court.

Information about a state's unemployment program is available in a local employment security or Job Service office, which is listed in the telephone directory.

Job Loss Because of Foreign Imports

Workers who are totally or partially unemployed because of foreign import competition may be eligible for help under the federal government's Trade Adjustment Assistance (TAA) program. This assistance includes cash benefits not to exceed $600, retraining, relocation allowance, and additional unemployment compensation when a worker's regular unemployment pay runs out.

Applications (petitions) are available at local employment security or Job Service offices and may be filed by three or more workers or their representative. The completed application should be sent to:

Office of Trade Adjustment Assistance
Employment and Training Administration
U.S. Department of Labor
601 D Street, N.W.
Washington, D.C. 20213

Disaster-Caused Job Loss

A worker whose employment has been lost or interrupted as a direct result of a major disaster—e.g., hurricane, tornado, flood, or earthquake—which the President determines warrants federal assistance to communities and individuals may be eligible for special Disaster Unemployment Assistance (DUA).

An application for DUA is made at the local employment security or Job Service office. The amount of the DUA benefit is based on the amount of unemployment compensation the state pays, with the DUA benefit being reduced to the extent the worker receives regular unemployment pay or other forms of income protection.

10

DISABILITY BENEFITS

The two principal programs providing financial assistance to persons unable to work because of a disability caused by a physical or mental illness or injury are Social Security and workers' compensation. Social Security benefits are provided through a federal program to persons unable to work because of an injury or illness regardless of whether it is job-related. Workers' compensation programs, which are operated by the states, provide benefits to workers unable to work because of a job-related injury.

The two programs define disability differently. Workers' compensation programs generally define disability as a person's inability to perform his or her past regular or customary work, while the Social Security law defines disability as a person's inability not only to perform past work, but also their inability to perform any other substantial and gainful work.

There are also special disability programs for coal miners, military veterans, and law enforcement officials.

SOCIAL SECURITY DISABILITY BENEFITS

Insured Status

In order for workers to be eligible for Social Security Disability benefits they must be under 65 years of age and have a physical or mental impairment that prevents them from working for at least 12 months. They must also be "insured."

A worker becomes insured by working long enough and recently enough under Social Security to earn sufficient credits for eligibility for disability benefits. These credits are earned when contributions—taxes—are deducted from the worker's pay by the employer and paid into a special Social Security fund. The employer contributes an equal amount. A worker who is self-employed pays directly into Social Security. (These payments are also used to fund Social Security's retirement system, which is covered in Chapter 22.)

The amount of credit a worker needs to become insured depends on the worker's age at the time disability begins:

- Workers becoming disabled before reaching age 24 are insured if they have worked 1½ years under Social Security in the three-year period before the disability begins.

- Workers 24 through 30 years of age are insured if they have worked half the time under Social Security between age 21 and the time they become disabled.

- Workers 31 years old or older are insured if they have worked at least five years under Social Security in the 10-year period ending when they become disabled, and have also worked overall under Social Security for a minimum number of years, depending on their age at the time the disability begins. The following chart shows the years of credit that are needed.

Persons born after 1929 and becoming disabled at age	Persons born before 1930 and becoming disabled before 62 in	Years of work needed
42 or younger		5
44		5½
46		6
48		6½
50		7
52		7½
53		7¾
54	1983	8
55	1984	8¼
56	1985	8½
58	1987	9
60	1989	9½
62 or older	1991 or later	10

Disability Determination

If a worker applying for disability benefits—referred to by the Social Security Administration as a "claimant"—is insured, the next step is to determine whether the worker is disabled. This determination will be based on a review of the information from doctors, hospitals, clinics, or other institutions that have provided treatment for the worker's condition. The worker may also be asked to undergo additional examinations or tests at government expense in order to determine the severity of the condition. The worker, however, has the burden of showing that he or she is disabled and should therefore submit in support of the claim all the medical information relating to the alleged disabling condition.

Social Security's rules for determining whether a person is disabled are generally more stringent than those of other government and private disability programs. The Social Security Administration therefore does not necessarily find that a person is disabled because he or she was found to be disabled under workers' compensation or any other disability program. To be considered disabled under Social Security law a person must not only be unable to perform past work, but must also be unable to perform any other substantial and gainful work activity.

A doctor's opinion that a worker is "disabled" is also not binding on the Social Security Administration. The Social Security Administration will, however, look at the doctor's medical findings concerning the extent to which the person's condition limits the ability to engage in activities necessary for work. It will then determine, on the basis of all the evidence, whether the person is so limited by a severe physical or mental condition that he or she would be unable to engage in any work activity.

Should the medical condition prevent the worker from performing past work, the Social Security Administration will take into account the person's age, education, and work experience as well as the physical or mental limitations imposed by the condition in deciding whether there are any other jobs the person can perform. When insured workers are found to be unable to do their past work or any other work, and the severity of the condition has lasted or can be expected to last for at least 12 months, or result in death, they will be found to be disabled.

Payment of Benefits

Workers applying for disability benefits will receive a written notice from the Social Security Administration advising them whether or not the claim has been approved. If approved, the notice will show the amount of monthly benefits to be received. Benefits, however, do not begin until after the disability has lasted for five months. If the sixth month has passed by the time the claim is approved, the first check could include back payments for up to 12 months.

The amount of disability payments is generally the same as the retirement benefits the worker would receive at age 65—an amount based on the worker's lifetime earnings covered by Social Security. A monthly disability benefit in 1987 can be as high as $789.

Payments continue for as long as the person cannot work because of the disability. Most cases are periodically reviewed to verify that the person continues to be eligible for benefits. The worker must notify the Social Security Administration if the condition improves or if he or she returns to work activity.

Dependent Benefits

Dependent children of a disabled worker are also eligible for benefits. Dependent children include unmarried children under the age of 18 and unmarried children 18 years of age or older who become disabled before age 22 and continue to be disabled. Also eligible for benefits is the worker's spouse who is 62 years old or older, or who cares for a child who is disabled or under age 16.

Survivor Benefits

If a worker dies, his or her dependents may also be entitled to monthly benefits. Additionally, a lump-sum payment of $255 can also be made to an eligible surviving widow, widower, or dependent child.

Supplemental Security Income

Another program administered by the Social Security Administration is Supplemental Security Income (SSI). This program makes basic monthly payments to disabled persons and to persons 65 years of age or older who, in either case, have little income and resources (assets). For individuals the resource limit for eligibility for SSI is $1,800 and the income limit is $340 a month. For a couple the resource limit is $2,700 and the income limit is $510 a month. Personal effects or household goods valued at less than $2,000 and a person's home are not counted toward the resource limitation.

SSI is supported by general tax money rather than by money paid into the Social Security fund by workers and employers. A person eligible for SSI, including a disabled child, is not required to have worked to receive SSI.

Disabled workers and persons over age 65 who receive regular Social Security disability or retirement benefits may also be eligible for SSI if their Social Security benefits (which are counted toward the income limitation) together with their other income and resources do not exceed the limits for eligibility for SSI.

Appeal Procedure

A written notice is sent to a worker each time a determination is made on a Social Security claim. If the worker does not agree with the determination, he or she has the right to appeal. The worker also has the right to be represented at any stage of the claim by an attorney or anyone the worker chooses as a representative.

Briefly, there are four steps in the appeal process:
1. Reconsideration of the initial determination;
2. Hearing before an administrative law judge;
3. Appeals Council review; and
4. Federal court action.

Claimants have 60 days from the date they receive a notice at each step of the appeal to proceed to the next stage.

1. *Reconsideration.* A reconsideration, the first step in an appeal, is a review of the claim to determine whether the original determination was correct. Workers have the right to review their files and to submit any additional information that they consider helpful to their claims.

2. *Hearing Before Administrative Law Judge.* If the worker disagrees with the reconsideration determination, he or she may request a hearing before an administrative law judge who is independent of the initial and reconsidered determinations. This hearing is usually held in the same city as the Social Security office that handled the claim. At the hearing the claimant or a representative may question any witnesses, present new evidence, and examine the evidence on which the judge's decision will be based. The judge has the authority to require that vocational or medical experts testify at the hearing concerning the severity of the worker's condition or whether there are any jobs the person can perform despite the physical or mental impairment.

The worker may request that the judge make a decision without a hearing, in which case the judge will base the decision on the evidence in the file together with any additional evidence or statements that the worker may submit.

3. *Appeals Council Review.* If the worker disagrees with the judge's decision, he or she may request review of the decision by an Appeals Council, located in Washington, D.C. Should the Council decide to review the judge's decision, the worker has the right to file a written statement and to request an appearance to present oral argument. Most reviews, however, are decided on the basis of the written statement and the evidence in the file without oral argument.

4. *Federal Court Action.* If the worker believes that the Council's decision is not correct, or if the Council declines to review the case, the worker may bring suit in a federal district court within 60 days of the date the notice of the Council's decision or denial of review was mailed.

Requests for reconsideration, a hearing, or Appeals Council review must be in writing and filed with any Social Security office by the worker or by a representative. The necessary forms are available in these offices and the people there will help a worker complete the forms.

Social Security offices, which are listed in the telephone directory, also have a wide variety of publications available to workers and the public, explaining all aspects of the Social Security system and its disability and retirement programs.

WORKERS' COMPENSATION DISABILITY BENEFITS

All states have workers' compensation systems that provide replacement income to employees for earnings lost due to job-related accidents or occupational diseases. These programs do not ordinarily provide benefits for injuries that are not job-related. However, five states—California, Hawaii, New Jersey, New York, and Rhode Island—have separate disability programs providing benefits to temporarily disabled workers who do not qualify for workers' compensation. In all but New York, these special programs are operated by the state employment service. In New York, the program is administered by its Workman's Compensation Board.

No-Fault System

For employees with job-related injuries, and their employers, workers' compensation is a "no-fault" system: An employer pays benefits to the employee for job-connected injuries without regard to who was at fault in causing the injury, while the employee in return forgoes the right to sue the employer. However, if the worker's injury was caused by a third party—for example, because of a defect in a product or machine made by another company—the employee can collect workers' compensation from the employer and sue the third party separately for causing the injury.

Workers Covered

Workers' compensation may apply to both private and public employment, but no law covers all employees. In one state, coverage is compulsory only for "hazardous" employment, and some states exempt employers with fewer than a specified number of workers. Agricultural, domestic, and casual workers are also often excluded from compulsory coverage.

Depending on state law, employers required to provide disability compensation may obtain coverage by buying insurance from a private insurance company, by paying into a state-run compensation program, or, if financially able and legally permitted, through self-insurance. North Dakota and Wyoming do not permit self-insurance arrangements, and Texas permits only state and political subdivisions to self-insure. However, in three states—New Jersey, South Carolina, and Texas—employers can elect not to participate in the state's workers' compensation program. If they elect not to participate, they can be sued by their employees for job-related injuries.

Benefits

Workers' compensation makes payments to an injured worker for necessary medical expenses and, in the event of death, pays benefits, including burial expenses, to the worker's family. Many states also provide special payments, such as a lump sum for disfigurement, rehabilitation services to help the worker obtain new employment, or extra benefits for minors injured while illegally employed.

The amount of benefits an injured worker receives because of lost work time depends on the type of disability. An employee unable to work at all while recovering from an injury, but expected to recover and return to work, is considered to have a *temporary total disability*. Monetary benefits for this type of disability are usually based on a percentage of the worker's pre-disability average wages, which in most states is two-thirds of the worker's average weekly wage, but with limits on the minimum and maximum amount that can be received.

An employee unable to work at all, or unable to work regularly in any stable branch of the labor market and not expected to be able to return to work, is considered to have a *permanent total disability*. In most states a worker who is totally disabled receives benefits for life or for the period of disability. However, some states limit the total amount that can be received.

A worker with a permanent impairment that is not totally disabling—one that limits the ability to work to some extent but does not prevent a worker from returning to his or her old job or to another type of employment after recovery—has what is referred to as a *permanent partial disability*. There are in turn two classes of permanent partial disabilities: "schedule" and "nonschedule" injuries. A schedule injury is one that causes the loss of a part of the worker's body, such as an arm, an ear, or a leg. A predetermined schedule lists the payments to be made for a lost body member, with each state maintaining its own payment schedule. In Pennsylvania, for example, a worker losing a hand in 1987 would receive $120,935, while a worker in Colorado with the same loss would receive $8,736.

Nonschedule injuries are those of a more general nature, such as injuries to the back or head. Depending on the state, benefits are based on a percentage of the impairment to total disability, or to schedule injuries, or on the difference between the worker's wages before the injury and the wages he or she is able to earn afterwards.

Waiting Period

Most state laws require a waiting period of three to seven days following a disabling injury before the payment of benefits for lost work time begins. In some states, benefits are retroactively paid to the date of injury if disability continues over an established period of time. There is no waiting period for necessary medical or hospital care.

Claims Procedure

When employees are injured they must notify their employer and file for benefits within a specified period of time. Employers in most states are required to post notices informing their employees of these reporting and filing requirements. The procedure for paying claims after an employer becomes aware of an injury varies from state to state, but generally it begins with the employer reporting the injury to its insurance carrier and to the state's workers' compensation agency. If there is no dispute that the injury was job-related, the carrier usually accepts the claim and begins paying benefits. In many cases this involves paying only for the medical expenses because the injury caused little or no loss of work. However, if the time lost from work exceeds the waiting period, payments for lost work begin and continue until the worker recovers, or, if the injury is permanent, until an assessment can be made of the extent to which the worker is permanently disabled.

Disputes sometimes arise between the employee and the carrier over the payment of claims. When they do, they usually relate to such issues as whether the injury was job-related, the extent of the permanency of the injury, or, if the injury was permanent, whether the worker will eventually be able to return to the old job or to some other employment.

The parties are often able to resolve their dispute through a settlement agreement whereby they compromise their differences, with the worker-claimant releasing the carrier from subsequent liability in return for a monetary award payable in a lump sum or over a period of time. If they are unable to resolve their differences, however, the case is referred to an impartial examiner, referee, or judge (depending on the state procedure) for a hearing and a resolution of the dispute. Medical experts may be called by either or both parties to testify on the extent of the worker's injury, and vocational experts may testify on whether there are jobs available that the worker is capable of performing. All parties are entitled to be represented by lawyers and, if the worker receives a monetary award, state law or regulation determines the fee the worker's lawyer can charge.

Rehabilitation

Most state workers' compensation laws provide for rehabilitation services for injured workers who, although unable to return to their former jobs because of an injury, can obtain other employment with medical care, counseling, guidance, schooling, or training. The federal Vocational Rehabilitation Act also provides funds for federal-state rehabilitation programs operated by a state's vocational rehabilitation department or agency.

Reopening an Award

All states allow awards to be reopened for modification to meet changes in the claimant's condition, such as an increase, decrease, or termination of disability. Some states allow awards to be reopened at any time, while most set a fixed period of time (from 1 to 10 years) for reopening following an award.

Discrimination

The laws of most states specifically provide that it is unlawful for an employer to discharge an employee for filing a workers' compensation claim.

Although employees cannot be discriminated against for filing a claim, they can lawfully be terminated if they are unable to work because of a disability. Hawaii's law, however, provides that an employer cannot suspend or discharge employees because of a work injury unless the employees are no longer capable of performing their work and there is no other suitable work that they are capable of performing.

Employers performing work under a contract with the federal government are required to hire handicapped workers, including persons who have recovered from a disability but who continue to have difficulty finding employment because of their prior disability.

Second Injuries

Some businesses do not hire workers who have been injured in prior employment because of the concern that if the worker is reinjured the employer will be required to compensate the worker for the total disability resulting from both the new and old injuries. To meet this problem, most states have adopted "second" or "subsequent" injury funds. Under these arrangements, if a subsequent injury does occur, the employer has to pay only for the last, or second, injury. The employee, however, is compensated for the disability from the combined injuries with the additional compensation being paid from the state-supported second injury fund.

More information on a state's workers' compensation system can be obtained from a state labor department listed in the Appendices. The Chamber of Commerce has also prepared an "Analysis of Workers' Compensation Laws." Address inquiries about the publication to:

Chamber of Commerce of the United States
1615 H Street, N.W.
Washington, D.C. 20062

VETERANS' DISABILITY BENEFITS

Service-Connected Injuries

Veterans with a physical or mental disability caused by military service may be eligible for a service-connected pension. Payments are based on a percentage of the disability according to the Veterans Administration's schedule for rating disabilities and are paid to the veteran regardless of any other income the veteran may have.

Nonservice Injuries

Veterans with disabilities that are not service-connected may be eligible for pensions if they are 100 percent disabled regardless of whether their disabilities are related to military service.

Unlike a service-connected disability, however, compensation for a nonservice impairment is an aid payment and is reduced in accordance with a veteran's other income. The veteran must also have served in the military service during specified periods of time and received a discharge under other than dishonorable conditions after 90 or more days of military service.

The Veterans Administration and private organizations such as the Disabled American Veterans can provide more information to veterans applying for benefits.

OTHER DISABILITY BENEFITS

Black Lung Disability Benefits

The federal Black Lung Benefits Reform Act provides for the payment of monthly cash benefits to coal miners who are totally disabled because of pneumoconiosis ("black lung"). Benefits are also payable to the miner's dependent spouse, divorced spouse, and children, and are also payable to surviving dependents of a miner who dies while disabled because of pneumoconiosis.

To be entitled to black lung benefits, the coal miner must:

- Be totally disabled by pneumoconiosis;
- Have pneumoconiosis as a result of employment in a coal mine; and
- File a timely application for benefits.

A miner is considered disabled if, because of pneumoconiosis, he or she is unable to engage in comparable and gainful work. Comparable and gainful work is work in the miner's immediate area of residence requiring skills and abilities comparable to those of any work in a mine or mines in which the miner previously worked.

Applications for benefits can be made in any Social Security office, which will provide the information needed to establish a disability claim. An applicant whose claim is denied is entitled to a hearing before a U.S. Department of Labor administrative law judge.

Benefits for Law Enforcement Officers

State and local (nonfederal) law enforcement officers who are injured while trying to prevent the commission of a crime against the United States or while apprehending a person who has committed a crime against the United States are eligible for federal disability benefits. Benefits are also payable to the officer's survivors in the event of death.

The benefit amount is generally the difference between the disability compensation received by state and local law enforcement officers and that received by federal officers. The agency to contact for these benefits, or for more information, is:

Office of Workers' Compensation Programs
U.S. Department of Labor
Washington, D.C. 20211

11

EQUAL EMPLOYMENT OPPORTUNITY

Equal employment opportunity (EEO) laws are intended to protect certain classes of persons from discrimination in employment because of their social characteristics. The federal government, most states, and even many localities have adopted anti-discrimination measures. In some jurisdictions, these laws are referred to as "fair employment practices" or "human relations," but, regardless of what they are called, their purpose is to provide nondiscriminatory equal employment opportunity for the classes of persons identified in the law. For simplicity, they will be referred to here as EEO laws.

The first EEO law—in New York in 1945— prohibited discrimination on the basis of a person's race or color. In the last 20 years, however, the classes of protected persons have been greatly expanded by lawmakers. Federal EEO laws, for example, now cover, in addition to race and color, religion, sex, nationality, age (40 and older), the handicapped, and certain veterans, while some states and localities have expanded the protected classes even further to prohibit discrimination on such grounds as a person's sexual preference or criminal record. The District of Columbia's EEO law identifies 13 classes of persons protected by its law.

A summary of the types of discrimination prohibited by the states and the District of Columbia appears on page 62.

Equal Employment Opportunity Commission

A law enacted after the Civil War, the Civil Rights Act of 1866, has been interpreted to allow persons to sue employers in federal court for employment discrimination based on race, ancestry, or ethnic characteristics. But the principal federal employment discrimination law is Title VII of the 1964 Civil Rights Act, which makes it illegal to discriminate in employment on the basis of a person's race, color, religion, sex, or national origin. The list of "persons" protected by Title VII is extensive: Everyone from hourly paid workers to supervisors, managers, professionals, and executives are protected against job discrimination.

Title VII created the Equal Employment Opportunity Commission (EEOC) to investigate complaints of discrimination and to correct violations through conciliation or, if necessary, through court action. It also authorizes private individuals to bring lawsuits if their complaints are not resolved to their satisfaction. Independent contractors, however, are not covered by Title VII.

The EEOC has jurisdiction over all employers with 15 or more workers, labor unions with 15 or more members, employment agencies, apprenticeship committees, and state and local governments. See Appendix C for a list of EEOC offices.

Other federal EEO laws include:

- The 1967 Age Discrimination in Employment Act, which prohibits discrimination against employees or applicants for employment who are 40 and older.

- The 1972 Vietnam Era Veterans' Readjustment Assistance Act, which requires government contractors to employ disabled veterans and qualified veterans of the Vietnam era.

- The 1973 Vocational Rehabilitation Act, which requires employers having contracts with the federal government to employ and promote qualified handicapped persons.

The Age Discrimination in Employment Act is enforced by the EEOC. The Veterans' and Vocational Rehabilitation EEO laws are enforced by the Labor Department's Office of Federal Contract Compliance Programs.

Prohibited Discrimination

Under Title VII there can be no discrimination in hiring, firing, or promotions, or in pay or benefits, on the basis of a person's race, color, religion, sex, national origin, or age. This includes—but is not limited to—overtime pay, shift premium, job assignments, training opportunities, advancement, holiday pay, commissions, leaves of absence, and insurance, retirement, and welfare plans.

Benefits paid to an older worker under an insurance, retirement, or welfare plan need not be the same as that paid to a younger worker if the cost incurred on behalf of the older worker is equal to that incurred for the younger worker. However, retirement benefits for men and women must be the same regardless of the cost incurred by the employer.

Title VII does not require employers to hire, promote, or retain workers who are not qualified and it does not prohibit employers from basing wage differentials for their workers on such objective factors as merit, incentive, or seniority, provided of course that there is no attempt to use these plans to discriminate.

Affirmative Action Program

An employer may voluntarily adopt an affirmative action employment program to increase the number of minorities and

DISCRIMINATION PROHIBITED BY STATE LAW

	Race	Sex	Religion	National Origin	Age	Handicap	Equal Pay	Arrest Record
Alabama								
Alaska	✓	✓	✓	✓	✓	✓	✓	
Arizona	✓	✓	✓	✓	✓		✓	
Arkansas							✓	
California	✓	✓	✓	✓	✓	✓	✓	✓
Colorado	✓	✓	✓	✓	✓	✓	✓	✓
Connecticut	✓	✓	✓	✓	✓	✓	✓	✓
Delaware	✓	✓	✓	✓	✓		✓	
District of Columbia	✓	✓	✓	✓	18-65	✓		
Florida	✓	✓	✓	✓	✓	✓	✓	
Georgia					✓	✓	✓	✓
Hawaii	✓	✓	✓	✓	✓	✓	✓	✓
Idaho	✓	✓	✓	✓	40-69	✓		
Illinois	✓	✓	✓	✓	✓	✓	✓	✓
Indiana	✓	✓	✓	✓	✓	✓	✓	
Iowa	✓	✓	✓	✓	over 18	✓		
Kansas	✓	✓	✓	✓	✓	✓	✓	
Kentucky	✓	✓	✓	✓	✓	✓	✓	
Louisiana	✓	✓	✓	✓	✓	✓		
Maine	✓	✓	✓	✓	✓	✓	✓	✓
Maryland	✓	✓	✓	✓	✓	✓	✓	✓
Massachusetts	✓	✓	✓	✓	40-65	✓	✓	✓
Michigan	✓	✓	✓	✓	✓	✓	✓	✓
Minnesota	✓	✓	✓	✓	21-69	✓	✓	✓
Mississippi								
Missouri	✓	✓	✓	✓	✓	✓	✓	
Montana	✓	✓	✓	✓	✓	✓	✓	
Nebraska	✓	✓	✓	✓	over 40	✓	✓	
Nevada	✓	✓	✓	✓	40-69	✓	✓	
New Hampshire	✓	✓	✓	✓	✓	✓	✓	
New Jersey	✓	✓	✓	✓	✓	✓	✓	
New Mexico	✓	✓	✓	✓	✓	✓		
New York	✓	✓	✓	✓	18-65	✓	✓	✓
North Carolina	✓	✓	✓	✓		✓		
North Dakota	✓	✓	✓	✓	40-65	✓	✓	
Ohio	✓	✓	✓	✓	✓	✓	✓	✓
Oklahoma	✓	✓	✓	✓	✓	✓	✓	
Oregon	✓	✓	✓	✓	18-65	✓	✓	✓
Pennsylvania	✓	✓	✓	✓	✓	✓	✓	✓
Rhode Island	✓	✓	✓	✓	40-69	✓	✓	✓
South Carolina	✓	✓	✓	✓	✓	✓		
South Dakota	✓	✓	✓	✓	✓	✓	✓	
Tennessee	✓	✓	✓	✓	✓	✓	✓	
Texas	✓	✓	✓	✓	✓	✓	✓	
Utah	✓	✓	✓	✓	over 39	✓	✓	
Vermont	✓	✓	✓	✓	over 17	✓	✓	
Virginia						✓	✓	✓
Washington	✓	✓	✓	✓	40-65	✓	✓	✓
West Virginia	✓	✓	✓	✓	40-65	✓	✓	
Wisconsin	✓	✓	✓	✓	✓	✓	✓	✓
Wyoming	✓	✓	✓	✓	✓		✓	

women in its workforce when a conspicuous imbalance in the employer's workforce is shown by the underrepresentation of minorities and women in traditionally segregated job categories.

Employment Selection Procedures

Title VII does not prohibit (as some states do) preemployment inquiries about a person's race, color, religion, sex, or nationality. The EEOC, however, frowns on such inquiries on the ground that they are irrelevant to a person's job qualifications and recommends that such information, which is necessary for filing EEO reports with the government, be obtained after a person is hired and that the information be kept separate from the individual's other personnel records.

When employers consider persons for employment or advancement, the EEOC requires them to avoid selection procedures that cause women or minorities to be "screened out." An employer's procedure may be unlawful under Title VII even though the employer does not knowingly discriminate against an individual if its practices have the effect of excluding disproportionately more women or minorities from consideration for employment or advancement.

If an employer, for instance, requires that applicants take tests to determine their job aptitude and more women or minorities fail the test, the test is considered discriminatory. In this circumstance the employer must prove that the test is "job-related," that is, it accurately predicts successful performance in the job for which the test is used. Even then, it may still have to be discontinued if the EEOC or a complaining party can show that there are other procedures that would accomplish the same goal with less discriminatory impact.

Similarly, because educational requirements often disqualify a substantially higher rate of blacks than whites, it is unlawful for an employer to specify a high school education as a job requirement unless it can show that such a requirement is significantly related to successful job performance.

Minimum weight and height requirements may also be unlawful if they screen out women or minority applicants (such as Hispanic or Asian Americans) and the employer is unable to show that the requirement is necessary for the safe and efficient operation of the job in question.

In short, when employers have an employment practice that appears fair on its face but has a discriminatory effect, they must show that the practice is necessary for the safe and efficient operation of the business and that there are no alternative practices that would have a less discriminatory impact.

Arrests and Convictions

A potentially unlawful practice under Title VII is to ask an applicant about any arrests or convictions. Because members of some minority groups are arrested and convicted more often than whites, a personnel decision on the basis of an arrest or conviction record has a disproportionate effect on a job applicant from these groups. Employers therefore cannot disqualify a member of a minority group because of an arrest or conviction unless they can show that there is a direct relationship between an applicant's arrest or conviction and his or her fitness for a particular job.

Thirteen states have also enacted laws prohibiting discrimination against persons with arrest or conviction records and four—California, Illinois, Michigan, and New York—prohibit employers from asking job applicants about arrests.

In some circumstances this prohibition can present a conflict under state law where an employer must check the background of persons applying for positions where they will have access to another person's dwelling (see Chapter 5). Conduct leading to a person's arrest, even though it did not result in a conviction, may still demonstrate that the person would not be a safe risk for a job where he or she would have access to another person's home or apartment. The EEOC, as noted, does permit an employer to consider arrests and convictions in determining a person's fitness for certain types of positions.

Race and Color Discrimination

Title VII applies across-the-board to any form of discrimination by employers against an applicant for employment because of race or color. There are no exceptions. A black applicant who is qualified must be given the same consideration for the job as any other qualified applicant.

Whites as well as blacks are protected by Title VII. Giving preferential treatment to blacks, referred to as "reverse discrimination," is unlawful. However, where minorities or women are underrepresented in a particular job classification, it is permissible for an employer to voluntarily take steps to see that more minorities or women are hired to increase their proportionate share of the jobs.

Government contractors must not only comply with Title VII; they are also required by the Office of Federal Contract Compliance Programs to identify those jobs in which women and minorities are underrepresented and to adopt written affirmative action programs stating the steps they will take to recruit and hire women and minorities to increase their numbers in these positions.

National Origin Discrimination

National origin discrimination is the denial of equal job opportunities to a person because of place of origin, or the origin of the person's ancestors, or because the person has a physical, cultural, or speech characteristic of a national origin group.

An example of national origin discrimination, mentioned before, occurs when an Hispanic or Asian American is denied employment because of a height or weight requirement that is not based on business necessity.

National origin discrimination can also occur when an employer allows ethnic slurs to take place in the workplace, or requires that English be spoken at all times in the workplace. It is permissible, however, to require that English be spoken at certain times when such a rule is justified by business necessity.

Religious Discrimination

Denying or limiting job opportunities to individuals because of their religious beliefs or not making a reasonable effort to accommodate a person's religious beliefs is discrimination based on religion. An employer, however, is required to make reasonable accommodation only to the extent that it does not create an "undue hardship" on the business.

A religious school or institution may legally require that the people it hires be members of its religion. It cannot, however, discriminate on the basis of race, color, sex, nationality, or age.

Age Discrimination

Under the federal Age Discrimination in Employment Act it is unlawful for an employer to discriminate against persons 40 years of age or older in hiring, firing, pay, promotions, fringe benefits, and other aspects of employment. It does not prohibit discrimination against persons under age 40. (However, some state laws prohibit discrimination against persons in other age groups.) The federal law applies to all employers with 20 or more employees and unions with 25 or more members.

Examples of age discrimination include:

- Indicating an age preference in help-wanted advertisements (such as using the term "under 40," or descriptive words such as "young," "boy," or "girl").

- Classifying workers in such a way that their employment opportunities would be adversely affected because of their age.

- Requiring a person to retire solely because of his or her age.

An employer may base employment consideration on a person's age when age is a reasonably necessary requirement for the normal operation of the business (e.g., hiring an actor for a youthful role).

Employers must offer workers 65 years of age or older the same health insurance coverage offered to young workers. Although a person still becomes eligible for Medicare at age 65, anyone who continues to work at that age has the option of either accepting at no extra cost any health insurance coverage provided by the employer or electing to receive Medicare.

Discrimination Against the Handicapped

The federal 1973 Rehabilitation Act prohibits discrimination against the handicapped. A handicapped person is any individual who has a physical or mental impairment that substantially limits one or more of the person's major life activities. This has been interpreted to mean an individual who is likely to experience difficulty in securing, retaining, or advancing in employment because of a handicap. A person may be considered handicapped even though recovered from a previous physically or mentally disabling impairment (such as a heart attack or cancer), but has difficulty in getting a job because of his or her prior disability. Louisiana and New Jersey also prohibit discrimination in their states against persons with sickle-cell anemia.

Employees suffering impairments resulting from the effects of a contagious disease have been held to be handicapped persons protected by the federal law. However, the U.S. Justice Department has said that it is not unlawful under this law for an employer to dismiss an employee based on the fear of the employee transmitting a disease like AIDS (Acquired Immune Deficiency Syndrome) in the workplace, if the infected employee does not suffer from the disabling effects of the disease. However, California, Minnesota, and Wisconsin laws prohibit discrimination against employees with AIDS.

The Rehabilitation Act applies to all employers with federal contracts of $2,500 or more and requires them to recruit, hire, and promote qualified handicapped workers. Contractors must also make reasonable accommodation to the physical or mental limitations of qualified handicapped applicants unless doing so would impose an undue hardship on the conduct of the contractor's business. The ban on discrimination against the handicapped is enforced by the Office of Federal Contract Compliance Programs.

Vietnam-Era Veteran Discrimination

Under the 1972 Vietnam Era Veterans' Readjustment Assistance Act employers with federal contracts of $10,000 or more must take affirmative action to hire disabled veterans and qualified veterans of the Vietnam era. They must also list their job openings with the Job Service, which gives Vietnam-era veterans referral priority to such jobs. This law is enforced by the Office of Federal Contract Compliance Programs.

Bona Fide Occupational Qualification

Title VII provides that an employer can prefer hiring persons of a particular religion, sex, or nationality if the preference is

based on a "bona fide occupational qualification" (commonly referred to as a "BFOQ"). Religion, for instance, might be a BFOQ
for a religious organization; a particular nationality, a BFOQ for
an organization promoting the interests of that group; sex, a BFOQ
for acting or modeling positions.

The EEOC and the courts, however, do not favor BFOQs. An
employer claiming a BFOQ must therefore clearly prove that religion, sex, or nationality is a genuine basis for preferring certain
classes of persons for employment. Race and color can never be a
bona fide occupational qualification.

12

SEX DISCRIMINATION

Although more charges of racial discrimination are filed than any other kind, a greater variety of issues arise in cases involving alleged sex discrimination. The types of problems the EEOC and the courts have had to resolve have related to job advertising, preemployment inquiries, stereotyping men and women as to the kinds of jobs they should or should not do, sexual harassment, equal pay, comparable worth pay, pension benefits, and maternity leave.

Job Advertising, Sterotyping, and Preemployment Inquiries

Preemployment inquiries or job advertisements that indicate a preference or limitation on the basis of a person's sex are unlawful unless the preference or limitation is a bona fide occupational qualification.

It is also unlawful to hire or promote men or women on the assumption that one sex is better than the other at performing certain types of work, or to label jobs as "men's jobs" or "women's jobs," unless, again, it can be demonstrated that sex is in fact a bona fide occupational qualification.

Unless the job in question is clearly one for which only one sex can qualify (e.g., an acting role calling for a man or woman), each applicant—man or woman—must be considered individually as to his or her ability to perform the work actually required. Neither men nor women are to be arbitrarily stereotyped as to the types of jobs they can or should perform, regardless of whether one sex has traditionally performed certain types of work. The EEOC, moreover, does not consider state laws that prohibit or limit the employment of women in certain occupations to be a defense to an otherwise established discriminatory practice.

A job application may ask whether the applicant is a male or female or a "Mr., Mrs., Miss, or Ms., " provided that the inquiry is made in good faith for a nondiscriminatory reason.

A personnel policy that restricts the employment of married women but not married men is considered unlawful. For this reason the EEOC considers preemployment inquiries on marital status or the number or ages of an applicant's children to be an indication of discrimination against women. When such information is necessary, as it often is for insurance, reporting, or other business purposes, the EEOC suggests that it be obtained after the person is hired.

Sexual Harassment

Sexual harassment covers any "unwelcome" sexual advance, request for sexual favors, or other verbal or physical conduct of a sexual nature directed at an employee by an employer or by its supervisors or agents. Such conduct is unlawful if submission to it is a condition of employment, is used as a basis for making employment decisions affecting the employee, has the effect of unreasonably interfering with the employee's work performance, or creates an intimidating, hostile, or offensive work atmosphere.

An employer may be responsible for the sexual harassment of an employee by fellow workers, or even by nonemployees, if it knew or should have known about the conduct and failed to take appropriate corrective action.

Equal Pay and Fringe Benefits

Title VII prohibits discrimination between men and women with regard to their pay and fringe benefits, including pensions. Employers providing retirement benefits to their workers must pay equal benefits to male and female retired workers even though the cost to the employer of funding the program may be greater for one sex than the other.

A separate law, the Equal Pay Act, which was enacted a year before Title VII as an amendment to the Fair Labor Standards Act, also makes it unlawful to pay wages to members of one sex at a lower rate than that paid to members of the other sex for equal work in jobs that require equal skills, effort, and responsibilities under similar working conditions. The EEOC now enforces the Equal Pay Act.

Comparable Worth

Although some men and women perform the same work for which they receive the same pay, for various reasons men and women also continue to be employed in different jobs, with the jobs held mainly by women tending to pay less than the jobs held primarily by men. When the difference in pay for these jobs is based on the different work being performed (i.e., different skills, effort, and responsibility), there is no unlawful discrimination.

Under a theory called "comparable worth," employees of one sex performing one type of job would be allowed to establish a Title VII sex discrimination violation by comparing their wages to wages paid other workers of a different sex performing dissimilar jobs and by showing that their work has the same value or worth to the employer as that performed by the other group. In other words, under the comparable worth theory, jobs that are equal in value ought to be equally compensated.

There is, however, no universal standard at present for measuring the relative worth of jobs. The comparable worth theory therefore has not been generally adopted yet as a basis for establishing a Title VII violation.

Pregnancy and Maternity Leave

A woman cannot be discriminated against in employment-related matters on the basis of pregnancy, childbirth, or related medical conditions.

- A worker cannot be denied a job, or promotion, solely because she is pregnant. She must be judged on the basis of her ability or inability to work.

- A pregnant worker cannot be required to go on leave if she is able to do her job.

- Health insurance to cover expenses for pregnancy-related conditions must be provided to a pregnant employee if the employer provides health insurance to cover expenses for other medical conditions. Employers must also provide insurance for the nonworking wives of their male employees if they provide it for their female workers. However, they do not have to provide health insurance for an abortion except when the life of the mother would be endangered if the child were carried to full term. Health insurance must cover medical complications that arise from an abortion.

- If a pregnant worker requests maternity leave, she is entitled to it on the same basis that leave is granted to employees for other temporary disabilities. Her job must be held open on the same basis as jobs are held open for employees on leave for other disabilities, unless she has stated that she does not intend to return to work.

- After the child's birth, the employee has the right to return to her job when she is able to perform it if other employees who have been absent because of a temporary disability are also allowed to return to work. She cannot be prohibited from returning for any arbitrary predetermined period following childbirth. On her return she is entitled to fringe benefits and seniority on the same basis as other employees returning from leave for other disabilities.

13

EEOC PROCEDURE

The procedure for a person claiming to be aggrieved by an alleged discriminatory act, called an "unfair employment practice," is to file a charge first with a state or local EEO agency (if there is one) before filing with the EEOC. Sixty days later he or she can file a charge with the EEOC. (A sample of the EEOC charge form appears later in this chapter.) As a practical matter, the EEOC will often refer such a charge to the state or local agency and then, after 60 days, if the charge is not resolved, proceed with its own investigation. The addresses of state EEO agencies are listed in Appendix C.

An individual filing a charge with a state or local agency has 300 days from the date of the occurrence of the alleged discriminatory act to file the charge with the EEOC, or must file within 30 days after receiving notice from the state or local agency that it is terminating the proceeding. If there is no state or local agency, the charge must be filed with the EEOC within 180 days of the occurrence of the alleged discriminatory act.

After a charge is filed with the EEOC, the employer is notified and is asked to come to the EEOC office for a "fact-finding" conference to discuss the allegations in the charge. At the conference, conducted by an EEOC agent, both the individual and the employer are given the opportunity to state their views, with the EEOC agent exploring with both parties the possibilities of a settlement. Many charges are settled at this stage of the proceeding.

If no settlement is forthcoming, the EEOC proceeds with its investigation to determine whether there is reasonable cause to believe that discrimination has occurred. Its findings are then communicated to both parties, with the individual also being given a "right-to-sue" letter. The individual can also request such a letter 180 days after filing a charge with the EEOC regardless of whether the EEOC has completed its investigation and findings.

Court Action

The right-to-sue letter gives the individual the right to take his or her case to court. If the individual decides to sue, a complaint must be filed in federal court within 90 days after receipt of the letter. The EEOC may also bring court action, but actually does so in relatively few cases.

When a suit is filed the burden is on the individual, as the plaintiff, to prove that he or she was discriminated against. In most cases this burden is referred to as establishing a "prima facie" case. When the issue concerns a rejection for a job, for example, the individual's prima facie case would be established by presenting evidence showing that he or she:

- Was a member of a class of persons protected by Title VII;
- Applied for a vacant job for which he or she was qualified; and
- Was rejected for the position.

In addition the applicant must show that after he or she was rejected, the employer continued to seek other applicants for the job.

The burden then shifts to the employer to present evidence showing that the individual was rejected for a legitimate nondiscriminatory reason. The individual is then given the opportunity to present evidence showing that the reason given by the employer was "pretextual," that is, the employer's stated reason was a cover-up for a discriminatory reason.

Should the individual win, the court will usually order that the individual be given the job in question with back pay for any wages lost from the time of rejection. Attorney fees are also usually awarded in the court's discretion to the prevailing party. Courts do not ordinarily require complainants to pay attorney fees if they lose. However, there have been occasions where courts have required such individuals and their attorneys to pay attorney fees to the employer when the basis for the complaint was frivolous.

Retaliation

Under Title VII employers are prohibited from retaliating against any employee who files a charge or participates in an EEOC investigation.

More information about Title VII is available from local EEOC offices listed in Appendix C. The address for the EEOC's national offices is:

Equal Employment Opportunity Commission
2401 E Street, N.W.
Washington, D.C. 20506

For information about the EEO requirements for federal government contractors, contact:

Office of Federal Contract Compliance Programs
Employment Standards Administration
U.S. Department of Labor
Washington, D.C. 20210

CHARGE OF DISCRIMINATION

This form is affected by the Privacy Act of 1974; see Privacy Act Statement on reverse before completing this form.

ENTER CHARGE NUMBER
FEPA
EEOC

_____ and EEOC
(State or local Agency, if any)

NAME *(Indicate Mr., Ms., or Mrs.)*		HOME TELEPHONE NO. *(Include Area Code)*
STREET ADDRESS	CITY, STATE AND ZIP CODE	COUNTY

NAMED IS THE EMPLOYER, LABOR ORGANIZATION, EMPLOYMENT AGENCY, APPRENTICESHIP COMMITTEE, STATE OR LOCAL GOVERNMENT AGENCY WHO DISCRIMINATED AGAINST ME *(If more than one list below.)*

NAME	NO. OF EMPLOYEES/MEMBERS	TELEPHONE NUMBER *(Include Area Code)*
STREET ADDRESS	CITY, STATE AND ZIP CODE	
NAME		TELEPHONE NUMBER *(Include Area Code)*
STREET ADDRESS	CITY, STATE AND ZIP CODE	

CAUSE OF DISCRIMINATION BASED ON *(Check appropriate box(es))*

☐ RACE ☐ COLOR ☐ SEX ☐ RELIGION ☐ NATIONAL ORIGIN
☐ AGE ☐ RETALIATION ☐ OTHER *(Specify)*

DATE MOST RECENT OR CONTINUING DISCRIMINATION TOOK PLACE *(Month, day, year)*

THE PARTICULARS ARE *(If additional space is needed, attached extra sheet(s)):*

☐ I also want this charge filed with the EEOC. I will advise the agencies if I change my address or telephone number and I will cooperate fully with them in the processing of my charge in accordance with their procedures.

I declare under penalty of perjury that the foregoing is true and correct.

Date _____ Charging Party *(Signature)*

NOTARY - *(When necessary to meet State and Local Requirements)*

I swear or affirm that I have read the above charge and that it is true to the best of my knowledge, information and belief.

SIGNATURE OF COMPLAINANT

SUBSCRIBED AND SWORN TO BEFORE ME THIS DATE *(Day, month, and year)*

EEOC FORM 5 MAR 84   PREVIOUS EDITIONS OF THIS FORM ARE OBSOLETE AND MUST NOT BE USED

FILE COPY

14
UNIONS

A labor union is an organization that serves as a bargaining agent for workers by representing them in negotiations with their employer concerning their wages, fringe benefits, hours of work, and other terms and conditions of employment.

Unions are based on the concept that employees as individuals often lack the power to negotiate effectively with their employer on a one-to-one basis but can strengthen their bargaining position by working together through collective action. The right of employees to have a union represent them in collective bargaining with their employer is protected by the National Labor Relations Act.

Workers who want a bargaining agent to represent them can select an already established union, form one themselves, or even designate an individual instead of a union as their representative.

An organization can become a union and act as a bargaining agent even though it lacks a formal structure. An employee committee, for example, can be considered a union and serve as a bargaining representative if it exists, at least in part, for purposes of representing workers in negotiations and is not organized or dominated by the employer.

The area of employment law that involves unions and collective bargaining is called labor relations, a subject covered in later chapters. This chapter and the one following it deal with a union as an organization and the rights of employees as members of a union.

Local Unions

The basic union organization is the local union or lodge that represents workers in a particular area, plant, office, or other business facility. A local union, of which there are about 77,000 in the nation, can be completely independent of other unions or can be one of a number of other local unions that make up a national or international union. An international union is a national union with members in another country, usually Canada. Overall, unions represent approximately 20 percent of American workers who, collectively, are sometimes referred to as "organized labor."

74

Local union officials, such as the president and secretary-treasurer, are elected by the union's members and, except for the larger locals, usually continue working at their regular employment while holding office, performing their official union duties on a part-time basis. Some locals employ full-time business agents to handle the union's day-to-day activities and assist with contract negotiations. Virtually all local unions have stewards, who are members elected or appointed to act as the union's unpaid agents in helping other members or workers represented by the union with any grievance they may have with their employer. A grievance in a union setting is a complaint by the employee that the employer is failing to follow some provision in the contract it has with the union.

Unions generally require new members to pay an initiation fee and sometimes may impose special assessments on their members, but their principal means of financial support are the dues paid by union members.

Reporting Requirements

As noted before, a union can be created to represent workers in collective bargaining without having any formal structure. However, once it becomes a bargaining representative it must adopt a constitution and bylaws that must be filed with the U.S. Department of Labor, together with an annual report covering such matters as the names and titles of its officers, their salaries and expense reimbursements; any loans it makes to union officers, members, employees, or business enterprises; its dues, fees, fines, and assessments; and its policies regarding qualification for membership, electing officers, calling meetings, disciplining members, ratifying contracts, and authorizing strikes. It must also comply with the requirements covered in the next chapter regarding the rights of its members.

International Unions

A local union becomes affiliated with a national or international union by receiving a charter from the international union. Delegates elected by members of the local unions affiliated with the international select the international's officers.

The international's constitution spells out the duties and powers of its officials, the rights and duties of its members, the procedures for the conduct of union business, and, generally, what local unions can and cannot do. It may, for example, require that the local obtain the international's consent before signing a contract with an employer or before calling a strike. If the local fails to comply with the international's policies, the international may place the local under a "trusteeship" and temporarily take over the local's operations.

The international, in turn, provides various services to its locals, which often include the payment of benefits to local union members during an authorized strike. The international also employs field representatives who assist local unions in such matters as bargaining, arbitration of grievances, and organizing nonunion workers through efforts to persuade them to select the union as their bargaining agent. The international's activities are financed by per capita dues paid by its local unions.

Some international unions engage in direct negotiations with employers, usually for national or industrywide agreements. Such contracts may cover multiplant operations of one or more employers.

Craft and Industrial Unions

Most national and international unions in the United States—but not all—are members of the AFL-CIO (American Federation of Labor-Congress of Industrial Organizations), which was formed in 1955 by the merger of the then separate AFL and CIO. Prior to that time unions affiliated with the AFL were historically those that represented workers with specialized skills or crafts, such as electricians, carpenters, and plumbers, while unions affiliated with the CIO, such as the Steelworkers and Auto Workers unions, organized and represented all workers in a plant or industry regardless of whether they were skilled or unskilled. AFL unions today are still often referred to as "craft" unions, while CIO unions are referred to as "industrial" unions.

A union's constitution also defines its "jurisdiction," that is, the types of workers it principally organizes and represents. This does not, however, restrict either an AFL or CIO union—or any other union—on the types of workers it can actually represent in most circumstances. A union has the right to organize and represent almost any appropriate grouping of workers, whether in a manufacturing plant or an office, and may lawfully attempt to displace another union as the employees' bargaining agent.

One of the functions of the National Labor Relations Board (NLRB) is to determine whether a grouping of workers is appropriate for collective bargaining. For purposes of allowing a union to serve as a bargaining agent, the NLRB requires not only that the union be willing to represent the employees in the appropriate group, but also that it demonstrate, usually through an NLRB-conducted secret election, that a majority of the workers want it as their representative.

Although unions generally have the right to represent any appropriate group of workers, there are a few circumstances in which a union's representation rights are limited. These include:

- *Plant guards.* The NLRB will not permit a union to represent plant guards if it represents other types of workers.
- *Craft severance.* Among other NLRB requirements, a union wanting to represent a group of skilled craft workers who are already represented by another union in a larger

industrial group must have had experience representing that type of worker before being allowed to carve out the craft workers from the larger group.

* *Jurisdictional work disputes.* When two or more unions at a construction project where a number of craft unions are working become involved in a dispute as to which union or group of workers is to perform a certain type of work, the NLRB will consider (among other factors) which of the contending unions has traditionally performed such work in determining which union-represented group of workers should do the disputed work.

AFL-CIO

The AFL-CIO is an association of national and international unions. Its activities, like that of many business associations, include promoting laws that it favors and providing various services for its members. Its leaders are selected by delegates from its affiliated national and international unions, which also pay per capita dues to the AFL-CIO to support its activities.

In all states and in the larger cities, unions affiliated with the AFL-CIO belong to central labor councils that coordinate their efforts on legislative issues and other matters that concern them on the state and local level.

15

RIGHTS OF UNION MEMBERS

A union's affairs are extensively regulated by federal law. A union is prohibited by civil rights legislation from discriminating against its members or the employees it represents because of their race, color, religion, sex, national origin, or age. A union's workplace activities in organizing and representing workers are subject to the NLRB's scrutiny. And as an organization its internal affairs regarding its relations with its members must conform to the requirements of the federal Labor Management Reporting and Disclosure Act (LMRDA).

One provision of the LMRDA, mentioned briefly in the last chapter, requires unions to file copies of their constitutions, bylaws, and annual reports with the Labor Department. Anyone can examine these documents, which are maintained by the Labor Department's Labor Management Services Administration (LMSA). Furthermore, a union must make these reports available to its members for examination and, for just cause, allow them to examine any books, records, or accounts that may be necessary to verify the union's reports. Under the LMRDA, a union member is anyone who has fulfilled the requirements prescribed by the union for membership.

Every employee, whether a union member or not, is also entitled on request to receive from a local union a copy of a collective bargaining agreement the local made which directly affects that person's rights as an employee. The employee is also entitled to examine at the local union's office any contract that the international has entered into that affects the employee.

Union members, however, do not have the right to ratify or reject agreements negotiated by their union unless given that right by the union's constitution or bylaws.

Other provisions of the LMRDA cover:

- Procedures for electing union officers;
- Responsibilities of union officers;
- Procedures for removing officials from office;
- Safeguards for the rights of union members; and
- Limitations on trusteeships.

Responsibilities of Union Officials

All union members in good standing are eligible to hold union office, subject to reasonable qualifications that the union uniformly applies to all its members. However, the LMRDA prohibits any person convicted of specified crimes from serving as a union officer for five years after conviction or imprisonment. Every officer or agent of a union that has property and annual receipts exceeding $5,000 must be bonded.

Officers are required to:

- Use the union's money and property solely for the benefit of the union and its members.

- Manage, invest, and disburse union funds only as authorized by the union.

- Refrain from any financial or personal activities that conflict with their positions as union officers.

A union member who believes that an officer is violating his or her duties can request that the union take action against the official. If the union refuses, the member can bring suit if, in the court's opinion, the individual has shown a reasonable basis for the suit.

FINANCIAL SUPPORT FOR POLITICAL CANDIDATES

The federal Corrupt Practices Act prohibits unions from using the dues money paid by their members to support the election of a person for political office. They may, however, ask their members to voluntarily contribute to an individual's election campaign, provided they advise their members that they do not have to make a contribution. The money that unions receive as a contribution must be kept separate from the dues money paid by their members.

Employers are also prohibited from requiring their employees to contribute to the support of a political candidate.

Electing Union Officials

Officers of a national or international union must be elected at least once every five years; officers of a local union must be elected at least once every three years. Unions may also hold elections at more frequent intervals.

The LMRDA requires that elections be conducted according to the procedures provided by the union's constitution. These procedures must in turn conform to the following federal standards:

- Secret ballots must be used in local union elections and to elect delegates who will nominate or elect officers of the parent national or international union.
- All union members have the right to nominate candidates for union office, vote for officers, and express their views on the candidates.
- Every member in good standing has the right to be a candidate and to hold office, subject to uniform and reasonable qualifications established by the union.
- Members must be given at least a 15-day notice by mail of the election.
- All candidates must be allowed to have an observer at each location where ballots are counted.
- Candidates must be allowed reasonable opportunities to distribute campaign material.
- Candidates must be allowed to examine the union's list of its members and their addresses.
- Union funds received from dues or assessments, or employer contributions, cannot be used to support any candidate.
- Election records must be preserved for at least one year after the election.

A union member who believes that any of these election procedures has been violated and that his or her complaint to the union about the matter has not been resolved can file a complaint with the Labor Department, which will investigate to determine whether or not a violation has occurred. If it believes that there has been a violation, it will file suit to have the election set aside and a new election held.

Removing Union Officials

Most union constitutions provide for the removal of an official who engages in serious misconduct. A member who believes that the union's procedure for removing an officer is inadequate can complain to the Labor Department, which will determine whether or not the procedure is adequate. Should the Labor Department determine after a hearing that the officer is removable, a secret ballot will be held to allow the members to decide whether the officer should be removed.

Other Rights of Union Members

Other protections for union members provided by the LMRDA include:

Equal Rights. All members in good standing have the right to attend and participate in membership meetings, subject to reasonable rules and regulations set forth in the union's constitution and bylaws.

Freedom of Speech and Assembly. Union members have the right to meet with other members to exchange views, arguments, and opinions, and to express at union meetings their views on candidates for union office. A union, however, has the right to adopt and enforce reasonable rules defining the responsibilities of union members, including rules relating to conduct that would interfere with the union's right to carry out its proper duties.

Dues, Fees, and Assessments. A local union may increase its dues and fees and impose assessments only by:

- A majority vote by secret ballot of the members in good standing at a special or regular meeting, after reasonable notice of the proposal has been given; or
- A majority of the members in good standing voting for the raise in a secret ballot membership referendum.

A national or international union may raise dues or fees or impose assessments only by:

- A majority of the delegates voting at a regular convention, or at a special convention for which affiliated local unions have received a 30-day advance notice; or
- A majority vote of the members voting in a secret ballot membership referendum; or
- A majority of the members of the organization's executive board voting for the raise if the board has such authority under the union's constitution and bylaws. This action, however, is effective only until the union's next regular convention.

Right to Sue. A union member has the general right to bring a suit or an administrative action against the union or its officers. A member, however, is first required to pursue reasonable hearing procedures provided by the union to try to resolve the matter before taking legal action.

Discipline. A union has the right to fine, discipline, suspend, or expel members for violation of its rules, but, except for the nonpayment of dues, it must first serve the members with a written list of the specific charges against them, allow a reasonable time for them to prepare a defense, and provide a fair hearing on the charges.

A union, however, cannot fine, suspend, expel, or otherwise discipline members for exercising their rights under the LMRDA. A member whose rights have been violated can file suit in a federal district court. It is also a criminal offense for any person to use force or violence against, or threaten, a member for purposes of interfering with the exercise of his or her rights.

Trusteeships

A trusteeship is any method of supervision or control of a local labor union by its parent national or international union which causes the local to lose the autonomy that it ordinarily is entitled to under its constitution and bylaws.

A parent union may place one of its locals under a trusteeship, but only in accordance with its constitution and bylaws, and only for the following purposes:

- To correct corruption or financial malpractice;
- To assure the performance of a collective bargaining agreement;
- To restore democratic procedures; or
- To otherwise carry out the legitimate objectives of the union.

The parent union is prohibited from transferring to itself the funds of the trusteed local union, except for the per capita fees and assessments the local normally pays to the parent. The parent must also file periodic reports on its trusteeship with the Labor Department. A trusteeship is presumed valid for not more than 18 months.

A union member believing that any of these trusteeship provisions are being violated by the parent union may file a complaint with the Labor Department. If, after an investigation, the Labor Department believes there is a violation, it may bring suit against the parent.

A member of the trusteed local union also has the right to sue the parent union unless the Labor Department has already done so.

For more information about the rights of union members under the Labor Management Reporting and Disclosure Act, write to:

Labor Management Services Administration
U.S. Department of Labor
Washington, D.C. 20216

16
UNIONS AND PROTECTED EMPLOYEE ACTIVITY

The Labor Department has the general responsibility under the LMRDA for protecting the rights of workers as members of a union. The National Labor Relations Board (NLRB), an agency independent of the Labor Department, has the responsibility under the National Labor Relations Act (NLRA) for protecting the rights of union members in the workplace. It also has the responsibility for protecting certain rights of nonunion employees.

Under the NLRA workers have the right to engage in union and other lawful activity for purposes of seeking changes or improvements in their wages, benefits, hours of work, or working conditions. Action by one or more employees seeking such changes through a union is usually protected by the NLRB. But for such action by nonunion employees to be protected, the activity must be "concerted"—that is, it must involve two or more workers.

The activity in which employees can and cannot engage, and what an employer can and cannot do in response, depends on the level and type of employee activity.

First Level: Action by One Employee

An employee in a nonunion facility may act on his or her own behalf, as many do, to seek a pay raise, better benefits, or an adjustment in working conditions. As a general rule, action by an individual worker relating only to his or her pay or working conditions, although lawful, is not protected by the NLRB. Employers may consider an employee's request and make a change or improvement, or they may lawfully refuse to consider the request and, indeed, since the action is not ordinarily protected, may even penalize the employee for the action.

Second Level: Concerted Activity by Two or More Employees

When two or more workers act together in a nonunion facility through a complaint, proposal, suggestion, request, or demand that the employer make a change or improvement in pay, benefits, or working conditions, or for their mutual aid and protection, their activity is considered concerted. When the concerted activity of two or more employees is for a lawful purpose (that is, an activity protected by the National Labor Relations Act), the workers are protected against retaliation from their employer. The activity of one employee may also be considered concerted if the employee acts on the authority of other workers and not solely on his or her own behalf.

Two or more employees also have the right, even in the absence of a union, to engage in a strike—which is a form of protected concerted activity—to back up their lawful request or demand. Workers engaging in a lawful peaceful strike cannot be fired. Their employer, on the other hand, is not required to consider the employees' request or demand (unless they represent a majority of the workers, as discussed below) and it can temporarily replace any employees who strike with other workers or hire permanent replacements for them.

As an alternative, the employer may lawfully discuss the matter with the employees or negotiate with them, or respond by making a change or improvement. The employer may also do nothing, and, in the following situation, it is in effect required by law to do nothing: If a union is currently engaged in trying to organize the workers, an employer cannot make any improvement in pay, benefits, or working conditions that it would not have made in the absence of union activity. Such action in the face of union activity is considered unlawful interference with the employees' protected right to decide whether they want a union to represent them.

Third Level: Activity by a Majority of the Employees

When a majority of the employees in a grouping of employees that the NLRB would find appropriate for bargaining participates in lawful concerted activity, they have the protection outlined above. In addition, if they select a union as their representative to do the bargaining for them, or form their own independent organization for this purpose, their employer is required to engage in formal negotiations with the bargaining agent they select. The usual procedure for selecting a bargaining agent is a secret ballot election conducted by the NLRB. See Chapter 18 for an explanation of appropriate bargaining units and the procedure for a secret ballot election.

When a union or an employee organization, or even an individual, becomes the employees' lawful bargaining agent as a result of a free choice of a majority of the workers in an appropriate bargaining group, it becomes the *exclusive* representative for all workers in the group it represents. The employer must thereafter deal *only* with the bargaining agent and no one else concerning any matter relating to the pay, benefits, hours of work, or working conditions of all the employees in the group. It cannot deal separately with any of the represented employees concerning any of these matters. The representative is the exclusive spokesperson for all the employees in the group for these purposes for as long as it remains their bargaining agent.

The represented employees are likewise required to channel their concerted activity on pay, benefits, and working conditions through their designated representative, but they retain the right to decide whether they want to continue to have a bargaining representative or to change representatives. There are, however, limitations on the times and ways in which this right can be exercised, as covered in Chapter 21.

LABOR RELATIONS LAWS

The National Labor Relations Act, enacted into law in 1935, gave workers the right to join unions and engage in collective bargaining. Also called the "Wagner Act," it created the NLRB. Section 7 of the Act spelled out the rights of workers to join and participate in union activities, and Section 8 prohibited employers from engaging in unfair labor practices that interfered with the workers' Section 7 rights.

Twelve years later the Act was amended by the Labor Management Relations Act, which was referred to at the time as the "Taft-Hartley Act." Section 7 was amended to provide that workers had the right to refrain from union activities as well as to engage in them, and Section 8 was amended to prohibit unions from engaging in unfair labor practices.

In 1959 Congress enacted another significant amendment to the Act with the Labor Management Reporting and Disclosure Act. This amendment, called the "Landrum-Griffin Act," prohibited unions from engaging in certain forms of picketing and established a code of conduct for unions for the protection of their members.

The National Labor Relations Act applies to most private businesses, but not to railroads and airlines. The labor relations activities of these industries are governed by the Railway Labor Act, which became law in 1926. This Act created a National Mediation Board to conduct elections to determine whether or not workers want union representation and to mediate disputes that arise during contract negotiations. The National Railroad Adjustment Board provides procedures for settling disputes in the railroad industry arising out of grievances or the application of contracts.

Unprotected Activities

Not all concerted activity is protected. Employees, whether union represented or not, lose the law's protection and may be disciplined, including being discharged, when the object of their activity is unlawful, or when they are insubordinate or disloyal, engage in violence or destruction of company property, or participate in an unlawful strike.

17
UNFAIR LABOR PRACTICES

The NLRB, as indicated in Chapter 16, protects the right of employees to engage in concerted activities for their mutual aid or protection and to form, join, or assist unions. It also protects the right of workers to refrain from any of these activities.

A violation of any of these rights by an employer or a union is called an "unfair labor practice." There are many ways in which employers and unions can commit an unfair labor practice. The following are just a few examples of each type.

Employer Unfair Labor Practices

- Discharging an employee for engaging in lawful concerted activities;
- Threatening workers with loss of jobs or benefits if they engage in concerted activities or join or vote for a union;
- Threatening to close the plant if the employees join a union;
- Questioning workers about their union activities;
- Spying on union meetings or even pretending to spy;
- Granting deliberate wage increases to discourage employees from joining or voting for a union;
- Taking an active part in organizing a union;
- Refusing to reinstate a qualified worker because the worker took part in a lawful strike;
- Refusing to reinstate an employee because the employee testified at an NLRB hearing;
- Refusing to bargain, or bargaining in bad faith, with an organization or union lawfully selected by a majority of the employees as their bargaining agent; or
- Announcing a wage increase without consulting the union lawfully selected by the employees.

Union Unfair Labor Practices

- Threatening employees that they will lose their jobs unless they support the union;

- Mass picketing that physically prevents nonstriking workers from entering the plant;
- Acts of violence committed either on the picket line or in connection with a strike;
- Entering into a contract with an employer to be the employees' bargaining agent when the union has not been selected by a majority of the workers;
- Entering into a contract with an employer that requires it to hire only members of the union or employees "satisfactory" to the union;
- Insisting on illegal provisions in a contract, such as a closed shop or a hiring hall that discriminates against nonunion workers;
- Picketing an employer to force it to stop doing business with another employer that has refused to recognize the union; or
- Asking workers not to work on equipment manufactured either by a nonunion company or by a company that has employees represented by another union.

NLRB Procedure

The process for determing whether or not an unfair labor practice has been committed starts with the filing of a charge with the appropriate regional office of the NLRB by a person believing that an employer or a union engaged in unlawful activity. (Samples of NLRB forms appear later in this chapter.) The charge, which must be filed within six months of the occurrence of the alleged unfair labor practice, can be filed by an employee, an employer, a union, or any other person. The NLRB, unlike some agencies that have the power to initiate action on their own motion, cannot file an unfair labor practice charge.

After a charge is filed, an NLRB representative will investigate the basis for the alleged unlawful activity, interview witnesses, and collect other relevant information. If the NLRB determines that the charge lacks merit, the charge will be dismissed. If, on the other hand, it finds merit, it will try to work out a settlement with the company or the union. Many charges are settled, but when the parties cannot settle the matter, the NLRB's general counsel issues a formal complaint against the alleged offending party—the company or the union as the case may be—and schedules a formal hearing on the complaint before an administrative law judge. The NLRB presents the case for the charging party at the hearing. The company or the union has the right to defend itself by presenting evidence in support of its side of the matter.

After the hearing, the judge issues a written decision stating whether or not an unfair labor practice was committed. Should the judge find a violation, he or she will order the company or the union to take appropriate corrective action, such as posting a notice where it can be seen by all employees advising them that the offending party will not engage in such unlawful activity in the future. In addition, if an employee was unlawfully discharged, the judge will order that the worker be reinstated to his or her job.

A party objecting to the judge's decision can appeal to the NLRB in Washington, D.C., which then issues its own decision in the matter after reviewing the record and the judge's decision. Any party to the proceeding objecting to the NLRB's ruling can appeal to a federal appeals court.

Although unfair labor practices occur most often in the context of a union organizing campaign—covered in the next chapter—they can, and do, occur on occasion even where a union has long been established as a bargaining representative.

The locations of the NLRB offices where charges can be filed are contained in Appendix B. The NLRB's address in Washington, D.C., is:

National Labor Relations Board
1717 Pennsylvania Ave., N.W.
Washington, D.C. 20570

GPO : 1984 O - 435-440

FORM NLRB-501
(8-83)

FORM EXEMPT UNDER 44 U.S.C. 3512

UNITED STATES OF AMERICA
NATIONAL LABOR RELATIONS BOARD
CHARGE AGAINST EMPLOYER

DO NOT WRITE IN THIS SPACE

Case	Date Filed

INSTRUCTIONS: File an original and 4 copies of this charge with NLRB Regional Director for the region in which the alleged unfair labor practice occurred or is occurring.

1. EMPLOYER AGAINST WHOM CHARGE IS BROUGHT

a. Name of Employer

b. Number of workers employed

c. Address *(street, city, state, ZIP code)*

d. Employer Representative

e. Telephone No.

f. Type of Establishment *(factory, mine, wholesaler, etc.)*

g. Identify principal product or service

h. The above-named employer has engaged in and is engaging in unfair labor practices within the meaning of section 8(a), subsections (1) and *(list subsections)* _____ of the National Labor Relations Act, and these unfair labor practices are unfair practices affecting commerce within the meaning of the Act.

2. Basis of the Charge *(be specific as to facts, names, addresses, plants involved, dates, places, etc.)*

By the above and other acts, the above-named employer has interfered with, restrained, and coerced employees in the exercise of the rights guaranteed in Section 7 of the Act

3. Full name of party filing charge *(if labor organization, give full name, including local name and number)*

4a. Address *(street and number, city, state, and ZIP code)*

4b. Telephone No.

5. Full name of national or international labor organization of which it is an affiliate or constituent unit *(to be filled in when charge is filed by a labor organization)*

6. DECLARATION

I declare that I have read the above charge and that the statements are true to the best of my knowledge and belief.

By _____
(signature of representative or person making charge)

(title if any)

Address _____

(Telephone No.)   *(date)*

**WILLFUL FALSE STATEMENTS ON THIS CHARGE CAN BE PUNISHED BY FINE AND IMPRISONMENT
(U. S. CODE, TITLE 18, SECTION 1001)**

GPO : 1985 O - 468-533

FORM NLRB-508
(8-83)

FORM EXEMPT UNDER 44 U.S.C. 3512

UNITED STATES OF AMERICA
NATIONAL LABOR RELATIONS BOARD
CHARGE AGAINST LABOR ORGANIZATION OR ITS AGENTS

DO NOT WRITE IN THIS SPACE

Case	Date Filed

INSTRUCTIONS: File an original and 3 copies of this charge and an additional copy for each organization, each local, and each individual named in item 1 with the NLRB Regional Director of the region in which the alleged unfair labor practice occurred or is occurring.

1. LABOR ORGANIZATION OR ITS AGENTS AGAINST WHICH CHARGE IS BROUGHT

a. Name

b. Union Representative to contact

c. Telephone No.

d. Address *(street, city, state and ZIP code)*

e. The above-named organization(s) or its agents has *(have)* engaged in and is *(are)* engaging in unfair labor practices within the meaning of section 8(b), subsection(s) *(list subsections)* .... of the National Labor Relations Act, and these unfair labor practices are unfair practices affecting commerce within the meaning of the Act.

2. Basis of the Charge *(be specific as to facts, names, addresses, plants involved, dates, places, etc.)*

3. Name of Employer

4. Telephone No.

5. Location of plant involved *(street, city, state and ZIP code)*

6. Employer representative to contact

7. Type of establishment *(factory, mine, wholesaler, etc.)*

8. Identify principal product or service

9. Number of workers employed

10. Full name of party filing charge

11. Address of party filing charge *(street, city, state and ZIP code)*

12. Telephone No.

13. DECLARATION

I declare that I have read the above charge and that the statements therein are true to the best of my knowledge and belief.

By _____
(signature of representative or person making charge)

_____
(title or office, if any)

Address

(Telephone No.)

(date)

WILLFUL FALSE STATEMENTS ON THIS CHARGE CAN BE PUNISHED BY FINE AND IMPRISONMENT (U. S. CODE, TITLE 18, SECTION 1001)

18

SELECTING A
BARGAINING AGENT

Union Organizing Campaigns

Although employees have the right to form their own union, workers who elect to have a bargaining representative usually select a local union affiliated with an established national or international union. This comes about in most instances as a result of an organizing campaign conducted by the union in which it persuades a majority of the workers in an appropriate group to vote for it as their representative in an NLRB-conducted election.

An employer, however, whose employees are the target of a union's organizing effort has the right prior to the election to try to persuade workers to vote for "no union," which is one of the choices presented to them on the NLRB election ballot. Both the employer and union, for that matter, have the right to resort to various forms of communications—speeches, letters, posters, pamphlets, handouts, meetings, and so on—to get their respective messages across to the workers. The ground rules for employer and union campaigning are set by the NLRB. Threats, bribes, and unlawful promises are not only clearly off limits, but are also unfair labor practices. Even conduct that is less than an unfair labor practice may be serious enough to interfere with the employees' free choice and may cause the NLRB to void the election and conduct a new one.

The list of what employers, employees, and unions can and cannot do during the campaign is extensive. To cite a few examples:

- A union can visit workers at their homes; employers generally cannot.
- An employer can call workers together on company time for a speech on its views on the union; the employer does not generally have to allow a union access to company property.
- Employees can campaign for or against a union during nonwork time (e.g., during breaks) and can distribute cam-

92

paign material in nonwork areas.

* Either an employer or a union can throw a party to have an opportunity to present its views to the workers, provided the refreshments are not conditioned on how the employees vote.

Authorization Cards

An essential part of the union's organizing activities is to persuade employees to demonstrate their interest in the union by signing cards authorizing the union to ask for an election. (See the example on the following page.) The NLRB will not conduct an election unless the union can show that at least 30 percent of the workers in the group want an election or support the union. A petition signed by the workers can be used for this purpose, but a union will generally ask employees to sign and date individual preprinted "authorization cards."

Example of a Union Authorization Card

```
                                    City _____
                                    Date _____
    I, the undersigned, presently employed by _____
    _____, do hereby designate Local Union No. _____,
    _____, of the International Union of Bricklayers &
    Allied Craftsmen, affiliated with the AFL-CIO, as my collective
    bargaining representative in all matters pertaining to labor conditions,
    wages and hours of employment, and
        (if not yet a member), I do hereby apply for membership in B.A.C.
    Local Union No. _____, _____, affiliated with the above
    International Union and agree to abide by all the provisions of the
    Constitution and By-Laws of said Local and the International Union.
                            Signature _____
    Social Security No. _____ Date of Birth _____
    Address _____ City _____ State ____
    Telephone: _____      Zipcode _____
```

Petition for an Election

After the union obtains the required worker support, it can file a formal petition with the NLRB asking it to conduct an election. (See the following page for a sample petition.) A petition can also be filed by the employees or even by the employer if the union asks it for recognition as the employees' bargaining representative. Unlike a union- or employee-filed petition, an employer petition does not have to be supported by employee signatures.

FORM NLRB-502

UNITED STATES GOVERNMENT
NATIONAL LABOR RELATIONS BOARD
PETITION

DO NOT WRITE IN THIS SPACE	
Case No.	Date Filed

INSTRUCTIONS: Submit an original and 4 copies of this Petition to the NLRB Regional Office in the Region in which the employer concerned is located. If more space is required for any one item, attach additional sheets, numbering item accordingly.

The Petitioner alleges that the following circumstances exist and requests that the National Labor Relations Board proceed under its proper authority pursuant to Section 9 of the National Labor Relations Act.

1. PURPOSE OF THIS PETITION *(If box RC, RM, or RD is checked and a charge under Section 8(b)(7) of the Act has been filed involving the Employer named herein, the statement following the description of the type of petition shall not be deemed made.)* **(Check One)**

☐ **RC-CERTIFICATION OF REPRESENTATIVE** - A substantial number of employees wish to be represented for purposes of collective bargaining by Petitioner and Petitioner desires to be certified as representative of the employees

☐ **RM-REPRESENTATION (EMPLOYER PETITION)** - One or more individuals or labor organizations have presented a claim to Petitioner to be recognized as the representative of employees of Petitioner

☐ **RD-DECERTIFICATION** - A substantial number of employees assert that the certified or currently recognized bargaining representative is no longer their representative.

☐ **UD-WITHDRAWAL OF UNION SHOP AUTHORITY** - Thirty percent (30%) or more of employees in a bargaining unit covered by an agreement between their employer and a labor organization desire that such authority be rescinded.

☐ **UC-UNIT CLARIFICATION** - A labor organization is currently recognized by Employer, but Petitioner seeks clarification of placement of certain employees: *(Check one)* ☐ In unit not previously certified. ☐ In unit previously certified in Case No.

☐ **AC-AMENDMENT OF CERTIFICATION** - Petitioner seeks amendment of certification issued in Case No. *Attach statement describing the specific amendment sought.*

2. Name of Employer	Employer Representative to contact	Telephone Number

3. Address(es) of Establishment(s) involved *(Street and number, city, State, ZIP code)*

4a. Type of Establishment *(Factory, mine, wholesaler, etc.)*	4b. Identify principal product or service

5. Unit Involved *(In UC petition, describe **present** bargaining unit and attach description of proposed clarification.)*		6a. Number of Employees in Unit
Included		Present
		Proposed *(By UC/AC)*
Excluded		6b. Is this petition supported by 30% or more of the employees in the unit? * Yes No *Not applicable in RM, UC and AC

(If you have checked box RC in 1 above, check and complete EITHER item 7a or 7b, whichever is applicable)

7a. ☐ Request for recognition as Bargaining Representative was made on *(Date)* and Employer declined recognition on or about *(Date)* .... *(If no reply received, so state)*

7b. ☐ Petitioner is currently recognized as Bargaining Representative and desires certification under the Act

8. Name of Recognized or Certified Bargaining Agent *(If none, so state)*	Affiliation
Address and Telephone Number	Date of Recognition or Certification

9. Expiration Date of Current Contract, If any *(Month, Day, Year)*	10. If you have checked box UD in 1 above, show here the date of execution of agreement granting union shop *(Month, Day, and Year)*

11a. Is there now a strike or picketing at the Employer's establishment(s) Involved?   Yes ....   No ...... | 11b. If so, approximately how many employees are participating?

11c. The Employer has been picketed by or on behalf of *(Insert Name)* ...., a labor organization, of *(Insert Address)* .... Since *(Month, Day, Year)*

12. Organizations or individuals other than Petitioner *(and other than those named in items 8 and 11c)* which have claimed recognition as representatives and other organizations and individuals known to have a representative interest in any employees in unit described in item 5, above. *(If none, so state)*

Name	Affiliation	Address	Date of Claim *(Required only if Petition is filed by Employer)*

I declare that I have read the above petition and that the statements are true to the best of my knowledge and belief.

_____
(Name of Petitioner and Affiliation, if any)

By _____   _____
(Signature of Representative or person filing petition)   *(Title, if any)*

Address _____   _____
(Street and number, city, State, and ZIP Code)   *(Telephone Number)*

WILLFUL FALSE STATEMENTS ON THIS PETITION CAN BE PUNISHED BY FINE AND IMPRISONMENT (U. S. CODE, TITLE 18, SECTION 1001)

An employer may also lawfully recognize a union without an election if the union proves that it is supported by a majority of the workers. An employer may even be ordered by the NLRB to bargain with the union without an election if the employer engages in serious and widespread unfair practices that prevent the employees from making a free choice in deciding whether they want a union. In the absence of such unlawful conduct, however, an employer can insist that the union win an NLRB election before accepting it as the employees' representative.

NLRB Jurisdiction

When the NLRB receives a petition, it first determines whether it has the authority (jurisdiction) to handle the matter. It cannot conduct an election—or handle an unfair labor practice charge—unless the employer's business affects or can affect interstate commerce. There are, however, few businesses that do not affect commerce in some way. A radio station with listeners in another state, for example, is considered to affect commerce. Similarly, an employer affects commerce if it sells goods to another company in the same state that sells outside the state.

The NLRB's legal jurisdiction is therefore extensive and potentially covers most businesses. It has, however, limited the cases it handles by adopting monetary jurisdictional standards. Under these standards a company must do at least the following amount of business each year for its type of operation before the NLRB will conduct an election or handle an unfair labor practice involving that company:

Nonretail operation. Sells $50,000 each year to consumers in other states; or purchases $50,000 each year from suppliers in other states.

Office building. Has an annual income of $100,000, of which at least $25,000 is paid by other organizations that meet any of the nonretail standards.

Retail. Has an annual volume of business of $500,000.

Public utility. Has an annual volume of business of $250,000.

Newspaper. Has an annual volume of business of $200,000.

Hotel or motel. Has an annual volume of business of $500,000.

Radio, telegraph, television, or telephone. Has a total annual volume of business of $100,000.

Taxicab. Has an annual volume of business of $500,000.

Transit. Has an annual volume of business of $250,000.

Transportation Enterprise. Has an annual volume of business of $500,000 from furnishing interstate transportation services.

Private health care institutions. $250,000 annual volume of business for hospitals; $100,000 for nursing homes, visiting nurses' associations, and related facilities; and $250,000 for all other types of private health care institutions.

The NLRB will also assert plenary jurisdiction over employers located in the District of Columbia, and employers who have a substantial impact on the national defense. Other types of businesses may also fall under the NLRB's jurisdiction even though they do not fall into one of the above categories. The NLRB has no jurisdiction over federal, state, or local governments.

Appropriate Bargaining Unit

The employee group in which an election is requested must be "appropriate" for collective bargaining before the NLRB will conduct an election. In labor law terminology, an appropriate group is called a "bargaining unit." Generally speaking, an appropriate unit for bargaining is a group of two or more employees having the same or substantially the same interests in wages, hours of work, and working conditions, such as a grouping of production and maintenance workers, office employees, or craft workers. All employees with common interests must be included in the unit. Unless it conforms to this requirement, it is not "appropriate" for bargaining, and the NLRB, which determines whether a unit is appropriate or not, will not conduct an election.

Certain individuals are not considered "employees" for purposes of determining an appropriate unit and are therefore excluded from bargaining units. These individuals include agricultural workers, independent contractors, and supervisors. A supervisor is an individual having the authority to hire, fire, or responsibly direct the work of other employees, or having the power to make effective recommendations on hiring, firing, transfers, discipline, or promotions.

Election Agreement

When the employer and the union can agree on the time and place for the election and the employees eligible to vote, they usually sign an NLRB consent election agreement. If they cannot agree, the NLRB will conduct a hearing and, in a written decision resolving the disputed issues, will either dismiss the petition, if it finds there are reasons why an election cannot be held, or direct that an election be held at a time and place it sets.

Voter Eligibility

Only employees employed in the bargaining unit during the payroll period preceding the date on which the election was directed or on which an election agreement was signed are eligible to vote. But the following are also eligible if they show up to vote:

- Employees in the military service;
- Employees who are ill, on vacation, or temporarily laid off;

- Economic strikers (those striking over wages or working conditions) who are engaged in a strike that began within the past 12 months;
- Employees hired as permanent replacements for economic strikers; and
- Regular part-time employees.

Election Notice

Employers must post in conspicuous places in their operation NLRB-provided posters that notify the employees of the election, show them a sample ballot, and inform them of their rights. They must also turn over to the NLRB a list of the names and addresses of the eligible voters, which the NLRB in turn gives to the union.

The Election

The election, conducted under the NLRB's strict supervision, is ordinarily held in the employer's operation. As each employee enters the voting area, he or she is given a ballot by the NLRB agent, which the employee marks in the privacy of an NLRB-provided voting booth and deposits in a sealed ballot box. An employee does not have to tell anyone how he or she voted.

Both the employer and the union are entitled to have non-supervisory workers present as observers at the election to see that only eligible employees vote. An individual whose right to vote is challenged by an observer may still vote, but his or her ballot will not be counted unless it can affect the election outcome. The NLRB determines whether the challenged individual's vote should be counted.

Neither the employer nor the union is allowed to do any election campaigning in the voting area.

After the balloting is completed, the NLRB agent and the observers open the ballot box, count the ballots, and note the results on a tally sheet.

Objections to the Election

Either the employer or the union—depending on which one loses—can object to the preelection conduct of the other party by filing objections within five days of the election alleging that the conduct of the other party unfairly interfered with the employees' free choice. The NLRB will investigate. If it finds merit in the objections, it will order a new election, but if it finds no merit it will do one of two things:

1. Certify the results of the election, if the union received 50 percent or less of the votes (which means the union lost); or
2. Certify the union as the employees' bargaining agent, if it received a majority of the votes.

Whether the union wins or loses, another election cannot be held involving the same unit of employees for at least 12 months. If the union wins, the next step is for the parties to enter into collective bargaining.

The NLRB will, on request, provide information on its election procedures. Union organizing and election campaigns are also covered in *Organizing and the Law*, which is available from:

BNA Books Distribution Center
300 Raritan Center Parkway
C.N. 94
Edison, New Jersey 08818

19
COLLECTIVE BARGAINING

An employer has a duty to negotiate in good faith with a union lawfully selected by the employees as their bargaining agent. It is expected to meet with the union at reasonable times, enter into negotiations with an open mind, and be willing to reach an agreement. It is an unfair labor practice for either an employer or a union to refuse to bargain or to bargain in bad faith.

Negotiations usually begin with representatives from the union and the employer sitting down together for the purpose of having the union present its formal proposals or demands for a contract. The subjects that a union can put on the bargaining table for the employer's consideration and for mutual discussion are any matters relating to the workers' wages, benefits, hours of work, or other terms and conditions of employment. These may include, but are not limited to:

- Pay rates
- Holidays
- Insurance plans
- Safety practices
- Layoff procedure
- Recall rights
- Seniority
- Termination
- Promotions

- Union security
- Union dues checkoff
- Work hours
- Overtime pay
- Grievance procedure
- Arbitration
- Pensions
- Vacations
- Shift pay

The duty to bargain does not require the employer to agree to any union demand, but it does require the employer to at least consider and respond to any lawful proposal presented by the union. The employer may also make proposals which the union must consider, but which, like the employer, it does not necessarily have to accept.

Negotiations for the first agreement may be lengthy because, in addition to agreement on wages and benefits, the basic contract relating to terms and conditions of employment has to be negotiated. The employer and the union may each propose "form" contracts, but neither party has to accept any contract provision because it happens to be in another contract somewhere else. The parties have the right to hammer out every clause and provision that they agree should be in their contract. Everything to be included in the contract is negotiable.

The basic purpose of an agreement is, of course, to codify the parties' agreement on the employees' pay, benefits, and working conditions. The employer and the union, however, also usually want specific provisions in the agreement relating to their interests. An employer, for example, usually wants a "management rights" clause that specifically recognizes the employer's right to run the operation, make business decisions, and direct the work force. A union generally wants a union security clause that requires that employees join the union and pay dues as a condition of employment and a provision for the automatic deduction— "checkoff"—of dues from an employee's pay. As with all other provisions, management rights and union security clauses are negotiable.

A union, as a service as well as an employee organization, incurs expenses as a bargaining agent. Its principal means of meeting these expenses is through the dues paid by its members and by the employees it represents.

As indicated in Chapter 5, 21 states do not allow compulsory union membership contracts, but checkoffs are permitted in all states. Moreover, even in states where compulsory union membership is lawful, workers do not actually have to join the union, although they can be required to pay union dues as a condition of keeping their jobs. Union-represented employees in health care institutions do not have to pay union dues if such payments are prohibited by their religious beliefs. They may, however, be required to pay the equivalent of union dues to one of three nonreligious charitable funds listed in the agreement.

Employees may, of course, voluntarily join a union even in a right-to-work state and, in all states, may resign from a union, although a union's constitution may impose reasonable restrictions on the timing of a resignation.

A checkoff clause—a form of wage assignment—allows, but does not require, an employee to have union dues automatically deducted from his or her pay. The clause must allow an employee the right once a year to revoke the checkoff.

Grievances and Arbitration

A clause found in most collective bargaining agreements is one providing for a grievance-arbitration system. Under this system workers who have a complaint that the employer has not followed the agreement on such matters as pay, promotions, or layoffs, or that they were fired without just cause or disciplined too strictly for an offense they committed, may file a grievance with their supervisor. If the grievance is not resolved at that level, the employees, with the union's assistance, are allowed to appeal to a higher level of management. Most systems provide for a three- or four-step grievance procedure, with the last step being arbitration.

If a grievance is taken to arbitration, the company and the union select an impartial person to serve as an arbitrator to hear and decide the grievance. The arbitrator's decision, called an award, is generally binding on both the employer and the union. A few nonunion companies also have arbitration systems for their workers' complaints.

Arbitrators are usually lawyers, law school professors, or other persons experienced in labor relations and arbitration. An arbitrator, however, can be anyone the parties mutually accept to hear and decide the dispute. The Federal Mediation and Conciliation Service and the American Arbitration Association will, on request, provide the parties with the names of persons who regularly serve as arbitrators.

Although a union is not required to take every grievance to arbitration, it must treat all the employees it represents fairly in deciding whether to submit a matter to arbitration. A union failing to provide fair representation to all the employees it represents, whether union members or not, commits an unfair labor practice.

Many employers, in agreeing to an arbitration system as a means of resolving disputes, ask for a no-strike clause from the union, which is a provision stating that the union will not engage in a strike during the life of the contract.

Stalemated Negotiations and the FMCS

If negotiations for an agreement come to a standstill—become stalemated—the parties are considered to be at an impasse. The parties are not required to continue meeting until one or the other changes its position on one of the stalemated issues.

When little or no progress is being made, either party may request the assistance of the Federal Mediation and Conciliation Service (FMCS), whose function is to help the parties with their negotiations. FMCS mediators, many of whom have had prior labor relations experience, are often able to get stalled negotiations moving again. Unlike arbitrators, mediators have no authority to decide disputes or to require either party to make any proposals or concessions. Nevertheless, through skillful maneuvering and tactful suggestions, they can often help the parties reach an agreement.

Strikes and Lockouts

A union can call a strike to back up its contract demands, while an employer can take equivalent action by locking out its employees. These matters are covered in the next chapter.

Final Agreement

After a final agreement is reached and any necessary employee ratification is received, the contract is signed by the parties and copies are made for employees in the bargaining unit.

The contract's duration, a negotiable matter, is generally for two or three years, but can be for as long as the parties want it to last. Sixty days prior to the termination of the agreement a party wanting to modify the agreement, or negotiate a new one, must notify the other party in writing and, 30 days later, if there is no agreement on a new contract, it must notify the FMCS and any state mediation agency.

As long as the union remains the employees' bargaining agent, whether it has a contract or not, the employer must continue to recognize the union as the bargaining agent and cannot make any changes in the employees' pay, benefits, or working conditions without notifying the union and negotiating with it.

Bankruptcy

An employer filing for bankruptcy can ask the Bankruptcy Court to cancel its contract with a union. However, before taking this action, it must first negotiate with the union in a good-faith effort to arrive at a mutually agreeable modification of the contract to improve the employer's financial condition. If the parties are not successful in reaching an agreement, the employer can then ask the court to cancel the contract. The employer, however, must continue to recognize the union as the employees' representative.

20

STRIKES, LOCKOUTS, AND LABOR DISPUTES

A strike or lockout results from a dispute or controversy between an employer and a union. Although disputes frequently arise when an employer and a union are unable to agree on the terms of an agreement, they can also arise in situations such as the following:

- The employer refuses to recognize and bargain with a union.
- The employer contracts out work performed by its employees to another company, or discharges or lays off its workers.
- Workers protest alleged employer unfair labor practices.
- The union objects to a company with whom the employer does business.

Every dispute, however, does not necessarily result in a strike or a lockout. Most disputes are in fact resolved peacefully, including most contract negotiations. But in every dispute or controversy there is always the possibility that one or both parties will escalate the dispute by resorting to pressure, rather than persuasion, to force the other party to accept its demands.

When this happens, pressure can be applied not only through strikes and lockouts, but also through picketing and boycotts. Picketing, which is usually accompanied by handbills, signs, or posters, in its simplest form is an attempt by workers, or a union, to enlist public support for their position by advertising their side of the dispute to other workers and to the public. Employees can engage in picketing without going out on strike.

As for boycotts, there are two kinds: primary and secondary. "Primary boycott," a seldom used term, is another word for a strike or work stoppage, which is in effect a refusal by workers to handle their own employer's goods. A secondary boycott, on the other hand, occurs when the workers apply pressure on the employer's customers or suppliers to have them stop handling the employer's goods or stop doing business with it. For example, when Company

A is involved in a dispute with its workers, it becomes the "primary" employer. If Company A's employees or their union should cause Company B's employees to stop handling Company A's goods or cause Company B to stop doing business with Company A, Company B becomes the "secondary" employer and the union's action in relation to Company B is a secondary boycott.

Lawful and Unlawful Pressure

Strikes. Pressure in itself is not unlawful. A strike for a lawful purpose is protected concerted activity. This includes strikes by employees, whether union represented or not, to obtain better pay or working conditions (e.g., a strike in support of their contract demands) or to protest an employer's alleged unfair labor practices.

Workers applying pressure on an employer by engaging in a lawful strike cannot be fired. An employer, however, can apply counterpressure by replacing strikers with other workers. If the strike is over pay or working conditions—which is called an "economic" strike—the employer can hire permanent replacements for the striking workers. When the strikers ask for reinstatement the employer must reinstate only those who were not permanently replaced, although unreinstated strikers are entitled to be placed on a preferential hiring list. A worker refusing to cross another union's picket line can also be permanently replaced.

Workers who strike to protest their employer's unfair labor practices cannot be permanently replaced, however. They are entitled to be reinstated to their jobs, even if their replacements have to be discharged to make room for them.

Workers also have the right to continue working even though their union has called a strike. A union member, however, who works during a lawful union-authorized strike can be fined by the union.

Lockouts. An employer can apply lawful pressure in a labor dispute by temporarily closing its plant and laying off—"locking out"—its workers. But it is unlawful for an employer to engage in a lockout to defeat the employees' efforts to form or join a union or to engage in other protected concerted activity.

Picketing and Boycotts. The law does not prohibit pressure through purely informational picketing at a primary or secondary employer. It is unlawful, however, for a union to engage in mass picketing that physically prevents nonstrikers from working, or to engage in picketing that is intended to be a "signal" for workers to stop work. It is also unlawful for a union to engage in picketing to force or require an employer to recognize the union as the employees' bargaining agent when:

- Another union has been lawfully recognized as the bargaining agent.

- A valid election has been conducted in the preceding 12 months.
- The picketing has been conducted for a reasonable period of time (not to exceed 30 days) and no election petition has been filed.

Another unlawful form of pressure occurs when a union engages in or encourages a strike for any of the following purposes:

- Forcing any person to cease doing business with any other person;
- Forcing an employer other than the one employing the union's members to recognize any union not certified by the NLRB as a bargaining agent;
- Forcing an employer to transfer work from one group of employees to another.

Timing of a Strike

Generally, a union can call a lawful strike at any time, with these five exceptions:

1. A union cannot ordinarily strike during the term of its contract with the employer if the contract contains a no-strike clause.
2. A union cannot call a strike during the 60-day period immediately preceding the expiration of an agreement.
3. When negotiations involve a hospital or a nursing home, the union must give the employer at least 10 days' notice of its intent to strike.
4. If the strike would cause a national emergency, the President can require that the strike be postponed 80 days while efforts are made to resolve the dispute.
5. Unions are generally prohibited from engaging in strikes against the government.

Unprotected Strike Activity

Employees who participate in an unlawful or unprotected strike may be discharged by their employer. Even workers who participate in a lawful strike may be denied reinstatement to their jobs when they engage in serious and unprovoked conduct such as:

- Physically blocking persons from entering or leaving a struck facility;
- Threatening violence against nonstrikers;
- Attacking management representatives.

21

CHANGING OR DECERTIFYING BARGAINING REPRESENTATIVES

Once a union becomes the employee's bargaining agent, the employer must recognize and bargain with it until some lawful event occurs clearly showing that a majority of the employees no longer support the union as their representative. This event is usually an NLRB election.

An election challenging an incumbent union's representative status results from a petition filed either by the employees seeking to "decertify" the union, or by a rival union or an employee organization seeking to replace the incumbent as the employees' representative.

The procedure for getting an election in these circumstances is the same as that discussed in Chapter 18, including the requirement that the petition be supported by at least 30 percent of the workers in order to have the NLRB agree to conduct an election.

If the incumbent union receives a majority of the votes cast in the election, it is again certified as the employees' bargaining agent. But should a rival union or an employee organization receive a majority of the votes, it is certified as the bargaining agent, thus replacing the incumbent.

If, however, the "no union" choice on this ballot receives 50 percent or more of the votes, the incumbent is, in labor terminology, "decertified," which means that it loses its right to serve as the employees' bargaining representative, and should a rival union or an employee organization also be on the ballot, it too would lose in its bid to become their representative.

Timing of the Petition

When a union is currently serving as a bargaining agent, the NLRB places the following limitations on the times during which an election can be held or a petition filed:

- An election cannot be held during the year following the union's certification by the NLRB as the employees' bargaining agent.

- If the union has a contract with the employer, a petition cannot be filed during the life of the contract, provided that the term of the contract is for not more than three years. A petition, however, can be filed during the 30-day period immediately preceding the last 60 days of the contract, or preceding the third anniversary of the contract, whichever occurs sooner.

- A petition can be filed after the contract has terminated, or after the end of the first three years of the contract, if a new contract is not negotiated before the petition is filed, or if the contract is not automatically renewed.

- A petition can be filed anytime when:
  — The contract does not have a specific termination date.
  — The contract has an illegal union shop clause.
  — The contract has not been ratified by the employees when ratification is required.
  — The contract is unsigned or incomplete.
  — The contract does not contain substantial terms and conditions of employment.
  — The contract can be terminated by either party at any time for any reason.
  — The bargaining unit covered by the contract is not appropriate.
  — The union is no longer in existence or is unwilling to represent the employees.
  — The contract discriminates among employees on racial grounds.
  — The union is involved in a basic internal conflict that creates confusion as to which union properly represents the employees.
  — The employer's operations have changed substantially since the contract was executed.

Employer Petitions

An employer can file a petition for an election when a union is established as a bargaining representative. But to actually get an election in this circumstance the employer must present objective evidence to the NLRB showing a basis for doubting that the union continues to have the support of the employees and that an election is therefore needed to resolve this doubt.

Before it will conduct an election, however, the NLRB must be satisfied that there is a sufficient basis for the employer's doubt about the union's majority status. If the NLRB is not satisfied, it will dismiss the petition.

Union Shop Deauthorization Election

A union shop deauthorization election takes away a union's power to enter into an agreement with the employer requiring the employees to join the union as a condition of employment. A petition for a union shop deauthorization, like other petitions filed by the employees, must be supported by signatures from at least 30 percent of the employees in the bargaining unit.

A deauthorization election can be held even through an existing contract would bar other types of elections. However, unlike the other elections in which the results are determined by the number of employees who actually vote, a union shop can be deauthorized only if a majority of the employees in the bargaining unit actually vote for the deauthorization.

Employer Conduct

Decertification and deauthorization petitions cannot be instigated by employers or their supervisors. Such action is an unfair labor practice.

22

RETIREMENT, PENSIONS, AND SOCIAL SECURITY

A pension is a system for putting money aside to provide workers with an income after they retire. The basic retirement program for most workers is Social Security, and for some it is their only pension system since employers are not required by law to provide pensions to their employees. Many businesses, of course, do provide some form of retirement income for their workers in addition to that provided by Social Security.

Although a retirement program, Social Security is not intended to replace all earnings a wage earner loses at retirement, and, indeed, may not provide sufficient income for many retired persons. As of January 1987, the average monthly Social Security check was $474.34. Workers therefore often supplement their Social Security payments with savings or investments. They are also allowed to continue to earn a limited amount of income from employment while also receiving Social Security.

Another federal program separate from Social Security encourages workers to establish their own personal retirement program by allowing them to make tax deductible contributions to an Individual Retirement Account (IRA). A worker can contribute up to $2,000 a year into an IRA if neither the worker nor his or her spouse participates in an employer retirement program, or, if either the worker or his or her spouse does participate in an employer retirement program, their combined gross income is less than $40,000. The same rules apply to a single worker except that his or her gross income must be less than $25,000. Money invested in an IRA account cannot be withdrawn before the individual reaches 59½ years of age without paying a penalty, unless the person dies or becomes disabled. An employer may also contribute to a worker's IRA in some circumstances. Banks, savings and loan associations, and employee credit unions will provide information to persons interested in creating an IRA.

Still another means by which employees can create a fund for their later retirement is through what is called a "salary reduction" or "401(k)" plan. Federal tax law allows employers to establish an investment fund to which their employees can voluntarily make tax deductible contributions through automatic deductions from their paychecks, with the employees being allowed to contribute more to a "salary reduction" fund than they can to an IRA. The law allows their employers to make matching contributions.

Self-employed persons can also establish their own IRA or establish what is called a Keogh plan, which allows larger tax deductible contributions than an IRA. A self-employed person creating a Keogh plan, however, must include his or her employees, if any, in the plan.

SOCIAL SECURITY

The Social Security retirement system, a federal program, provides benefits to retired workers, to certain dependents of workers who have retired or died and, as covered in Chapter 10, to disabled workers.

The system is financed through mandatory tax deductions from workers' wages. Employers pay an equal amount. Self-employed persons are also covered by Social Security and make their payments when they file their federal income tax returns. To qualify for benefits, a worker must have earned credits for a certain amount of work under Social Security. The amount of retirement benefits a worker receives is based on his or her level of earnings.

Applying for Social Security Benefits

Social Security benefits do not start automatically. A person who is ready to retire must apply for them. To receive full benefits a worker has to wait until age 65 to apply. He or she can start collecting as early as age 62, but the monthly benefits will be permanently reduced.

Payments to a worker retiring before age 65 begin with the month the person applies. A worker retiring after age 65 can generally receive retroactive payments for up to six months before the month he or she applies. Because there is a lag in processing a claim from the time application is made until payments begin, workers should apply three months before they want benefits to start.

Information Needed When Applying

When applying for benefits—which can be done at any one of Social Security's 1300 offices—the worker should bring to the office:

- His or her Social Security card or number;
- Proof of age;

- Form W-2 for the last two years or, if self-employed, a copy of the last two federal income tax returns. This information is important because earnings for this period will likely not yet be on Social Security's records and therefore will not be included when the amount of retirement benefits to which the worker is entitled are computed. Without this current information, it could take at least two years before these earnings are reported to Social Security and the benefits are recomputed and reflected in the worker's monthly check.

Amount of Benefits

Initial retirement benefits depend on the worker's level of earnings. These benefits increase automatically each year as the cost of living rises. If living costs increase 3 percent or more, benefits are increased by the same amount. A worker retiring at age 65 in 1987 can receive as much as $789 a month.

Individuals who return to work after they begin receiving retirement checks may, because of added earnings, become entitled to higher benefits. This is because Social Security automatically refigures benefits after additional earnings are credited to a worker's record. (But as noted in a moment, a return to work can cause a reduction in the worker's current check.) A worker delaying retirement after reaching age 65 also receives a 3 percent credit for each year delay up to age 70.

Continuing Work

A retired person, as noted, can return to work after starting to collect Social Security benefits. For that matter, he or she can collect benefits without stopping work altogether. However, the earnings of a person who both works and collects benefits can affect the amount of that person's Social Security check, depending on whether the earnings exceed an annual "exempt amount." If the earnings go over this amount, $1 is deducted from the monthly check for each $2 earned *above* this exempt amount. Only earnings from work affect an individual's benefits. Benefits are not affected by income from savings, investments, or insurance.

The annual exempt amount for 1987 is $8,160 for persons age 65 or older and $6,000 for persons under age 65. When a person reaches age 70, there is no limit on the amount he or she can earn.

An individual collecting Social Security who expects to earn more than the annual exempt amount should notify the local Social Security office so that it can determine whether some or all of the person's benefits should be withheld to avoid the payment of benefits that the individual may later have to repay. An annual report of earnings must be filed by April 15.

Medicare

Workers who are eligible for Social Security retirement benefits at age 65 are also automatically eligible to participate in the two-part Medicare program. One part, hospital insurance (Part A)—to which all workers contribute when Social Security taxes are deducted from their pay—helps pay for hospital care. The second part, medical insurance (Part B), helps pay for physician services. A monthly premium ($18.84 in 1987) is charged for medical insurance. A person applying for hospital insurance (Part A), which is available at age 65 whether or not the person retires, is automatically enrolled for medical insurance (Part B), unless he or she decides to reject it.

A worker who continues to work after reaching age 65 has the right to remain covered by any health insurance provided by his or her employer, with Medicare being a secondary source of coverage.

Dependent Benefits

Monthly Social Security checks are paid to certain dependents of a retired worker. These include:

- Unmarried children under 18 years of age or under age 19 if full-time high school students;
- Unmarried children 18 years of age or older who were disabled before age 22 and continue to be disabled;
- Spouse age 62 or older;
- Spouse under age 62 if he or she is caring for a child under age 16 who is receiving a benefit based on the retired worker's earnings record.

Death Benefits

If a worker dies, monthly Social Security benefits can be made to:

- Unmarried children under age 18, or under 19 years old if full-time high school students;
- Unmarried son or daughter 18 years old or over who was disabled before age 22 and continues to be disabled;
- Widow or widower age 60 or older;
- Widow, widower, or surviving divorced spouse of any age caring for the worker's child under 16 years of age who is receiving a benefit based on the earnings record of the dead worker;
- Widow or widower age 50 or older who becomes disabled not later than seven years after the worker died;
- Dependent parents age 62 or older.

Benefits can also be paid to a divorced spouse at age 60 or older or to a surviving disabled divorced spouse at age 50 if the marriage lasted 10 years or more.

Generally, a marriage must have lasted at least one year before dependents of a retired or disabled worker can receive monthly benefits, and a marriage must have lasted at least nine months for survivors to receive death benefits.

How Social Security Credit Is Earned

A worker becomes entitled to retirement benefits by earning sufficient credit through work, including part-time and temporary work, that is covered by Social Security. First, though, to receive credit, a worker (including a child who intends to work) has to obtain a Social Security number, which is a simple process of applying for a card at a Social Security office and showing evidence of age and citizenship, or immigration status. The number on the card is used by the government to keep a record of the individual's earnings from work. It is also used for federal income tax purposes. Only one number is issued to a person during his or her lifetime.

Employers are required to give their employees a statement of their earnings and the Social Security taxes deducted from their pay at the end of the year. In most cases deductions are shown on a W-2 form, which also shows the deductions for income taxes. The Social Security deductions are listed on the W-2 under "FICA taxes withheld." FICA stands for Federal Insurance Contributions Act, which is the law that authorizes the deduction of Social Security taxes from an employee's pay.

A worker's annual earnings for work covered by Social Security are reported by the employer to the government, which in turn credits the worker's Social Security earnings record. A separate record is maintained for each wage earner. This credit is referred to as "quarters of coverage," with four quarters equalling one year. Even though a worker may have more than one job, he or she cannot receive credit for more than four quarters in any year.

In 1987, employees and self-employed persons receive one quarter of coverage for each $460 of annual earnings they receive for work covered by Social Security. The amount needed to earn a quarter of coverage increases automatically each year to keep pace with the increase in the average wage.

A person who stops performing work covered by Social Security before earning enough credits will not receive benefits. But the credit already earned will stay on the record and the individual can add to it by returning to work under Social Security any time before or after reaching retirement age.

A worker with enough credit to receive retirement benefits is "fully insured." The amount of credit needed to become fully insured and eligible for a retirement check depends on the year the person will reach age 62, while the amount of the check the person will receive depends on his or her level of earnings over a period of years. The following table shows the amount of credit needed for retirement benefits for persons of different ages.

WORK CREDIT FOR RETIREMENT BENEFITS

Year in which worker reaches age 62	Years of credit needed
1987	9 (36 quarters)
1991 or later	10 (40 quarters)

A wage earner can check with the Social Security Administration to determine whether he or she is receiving credit for earnings by using the postcard shown later is this chapter. The postcard is available without charge at any Social Security office. Errors in a worker's earnings record can be corrected for up to three years. For further information and instructions on making a rough estimate of a wage earner's Social Security retirement check, see *Your New Social Security and Medicare Fact Sheet*, available from:

BNA Books
9435 Key West Avenue
Rockville, Maryland 20850-3397

Special Rules

Most jobs are covered by Social Security. However, there are special rules for coverage for certain types of workers, such as farmers, domestic workers, legal immigrants, and people who receive cash tips. Pamphlets containing information for these persons, as well as information explaining all aspects of the system for any person covered by Social Security, are available at any Social Security office.

Appeals Procedure

A wage earner who disagrees with a decision by the Social Security Administration concerning retirement benefits has the right to appeal the decision through the appeals process explained in Chapter 10.

PRIVATE PENSION PLANS

An employer is not required to provide a pension to its workers. But if it does, the plan must meet minimum standards established by the Employee Retirement Income Security Act (ERISA).

ERISA, a complex law, generally provides that if an employer has a pension plan based on age and length of service, its employees must be allowed to participate in the plan when they reach age 25 and work at least 1,000 hours in 12 months. It also requires that a pension "vest" after a worker has participated in the plan for a certain period of time, usually after 10 years. Vesting means that the plan will pay the employee a pension at a specified retirement age even if the worker should leave the job before reaching that age. However, a worker who leaves before the plan vests is not entitled to a benefit from the plan at retirement, although the worker is entitled to a refund of the contributions he or she may have made (but not the contributions made by the employer) to the plan.

	FOR SSA USE ONLY	
REQUEST FOR STATEMENT OF EARNINGS (PLEASE PRINT IN INK OR USE TYPEWRITER)	**AX**	
	SP	

I REQUEST A SUMMARY STATEMENT OF EARNINGS FROM MY SOCIAL SECURITY RECORD

NH Full name you use in work or business
First | Middle Initial | Last

SN Social security number shown on your card
DB Your date of birth — Month | Day | Year **A**

MA Other Social Security number(s) you have used
SX Your Sex — ☐ Male ☐ Female

AK Other name(s) you have used (Include your maiden name)

- - - - - - - - - - - *FOLD HERE* - - - - - - - - - - -

PRIVACY STATEMENT

The Social Security Administration (SSA) is authorized to collect information asked on this form under section 205 of the Social Security Act. It is needed so SSA can quickly identify your record and prepare the earnings statement you requested. While you are not required to furnish the information, failure to do so may prevent your request from being processed. The information will be used primarily for issuing your earnings statement.

I am the individual to whom the record pertains. I understand that if I knowingly and willingly request or receive a record about an individual under false pretenses I would be guilty of a Federal crime and could be fined up to $5000.

Sign your name here: (Do not print) | Date

I AUTHORIZE YOU TO SEND THE STATEMENT TO THE NAME AND ADDRESS BELOW: *(To be completed in all cases)*

PN Name of the addressee

AD Street number and name

City and state | **ZP** Zip Code

Form **SSA-7004 PC** OP1 (9-82) Previous Editions are Obsolete

This card, available at any Social Security office, can be used by a worker to request a free statement of his or her Social Security earnings record.

ERISA prohibits the discharge of workers to avoid paying them a pension. It also requires employers to give basic information about the plan to their workers and, if workers are entitled to a pension, to tell them how much they can expect to receive at retirement. ERISA, however, does not require the payment of any minimum benefit to persons eligible for benefits under the plan when they retire.

When a worker applies for pension benefits, the plan's administrator must let the worker know within 90 days whether the claim is granted or denied. A worker whose claim is denied must be given a written explanation and must be given 60 days to file an appeal according to the procedures the administrator must explain to the worker. A decision on the appeal must be made in writing within 120 days. If the claim is again turned down, the employee has the right to appeal to a court or to seek assistance by writing to:

> Pension and Welfare Benefits Programs
> Labor-Management Services Administration
> Room N-4659, U.S. Department of Labor
> 3rd and Constitution Ave., N.W.
> Washington, D.C. 20216

Simplified Employee Pension Plans

As noted at the beginning of this chapter, individual wage earners and self-employed persons can establish their own private pension plans. An employer can also make contributions to an employee's Individual Retirement Account in certain circumstances as provided by Internal Revenue Service regulations. When such contributions are allowed, the arrangement is called a Simplified Employee Pension (SEP) plan and does not require the employer to make many of the reports and disclosures of information that it would have to make under an ERISA-type pension plan. A bank or other financial institution can provide information on SEPs.

For more information about pension plans and ERISA, a lawyer or accountant specializing in such matters should be consulted because of the complexities of the law.

23
GOVERNMENT EMPLOYMENT

More than 13 million people work for federal, state, and local governments. Each of these levels of government operates its own employment system, with most using some form of "merit" employment, a system that, with certain exceptions, bases the selection and advancement of employees on their job qualifications rather than on their political affiliation. The principal exception to merit employment involves policymaking positions that elected officials can fill with persons whose decisions will reflect those of the official.

State and Local Government Employment

The National Labor Relations Act, the law creating the NLRB and requiring private employers to bargain with unions, does not apply to any level of government, although the U.S. Postal Service, which is a government-owned corporation, is under the NLRB's jurisdiction. A government agency, therefore, in the absence of other laws requiring it to bargain with a union (which some states and local governments have adopted), can refuse to bargain with a union seeking recognition as the bargaining agent for its employees. Government employees, whether union represented or not, generally lack the right to strike and can be discharged if they do.

Although not under the NLRB's authority, state and local governments are subject to the EEOC's jurisdiction and therefore cannot discriminate against their employees on the basis of race, color, religion, sex, or national origin. They are also prohibited from discriminating on the basis of age or handicap if they receive federal funds. The federal Fair Labor Standards Act ("minimum wage law") also applies to state and local government workers.

Federal Employment

The federal government, the nation's largest employer, employs almost three million persons through its civil service system. Federal employees work in many settings across the country and even around the world in offices, shipyards, laboratories, national forests, and military bases.

Most federal workers are hired through a "competitive" service procedure, which is a form of a merit employment system administered by the Office of Personnel Management (OPM), formerly called the Civil Service Commission.

A person seeking a federal competitive service job must file an application (Standard Form 171) with OPM. The qualifications for federal jobs are stated in bulletins or announcements that specify the education and/or experience needed and whether a written test is required. This information can be obtained from the agency with the job opening or from OPM.

OPM determines whether an applicant is qualified and, if qualified, gives the applicant a numerical rating based on his or her experience, education and training, or on the results of a written test if one is given for the position. Veterans may receive an additional five points and disabled veterans 10 points. The applicant's name is then placed on a list or register with the names of other persons who are also qualified for the same kind of job. Names are listed according to their rating.

When OPM receives a request for the names of qualified applicants from an employing agency, it sends the agency the names of the people highest on the list. The agency's hiring official then makes a choice from among the top three applicants. In some circumstances handicapped persons and disabled Vietnam-era veterans may be hired without competing with other applicants.

New employees in the competitive service serve a probationary period and can be dismissed during this time if they fail to perform satisfactory work. After the probationary period they become career employees and cannot be dismissed without evidence of misconduct, delinquency, or inefficiency on the job.

Pay Levels

Competitive service jobs are classified by grade levels based on the level of responsibility required for the job. Salaries correspond to the grade level; the higher the grade, the higher the salary. These grade levels are called "General Schedules" (GS) and apply to most white-collar jobs, starting with GS-1 and going up to GS-18. GS salaries are set by the President with Congressional approval.

Each GS grade has a set range of within-grade increases in salary called "steps." Employees performing adequate work receive step increases based on length of service until the top of the grade is reached. They can also receive step increases for exceptional work. However, step increases for managers and supervisors in grades GS-13, 14, and 15, and Senior Executive Service employees GS-16 and above are based on performance rather than on length of service. Senior Executive Service employees are those persons who are hired through competitive procedures conducted under the auspices of the employing agency to hold high-level positions in the agency.

Most blue-collar positions are covered by "wage order" pay rates that vary according to the location where the employees work.

EXCEPTED SERVICE

Although most federal workers are hired through OPM's competitive service procedures, the Postal Service, Federal Bureau of Investigation, and the Central Intelligence Agency are "excepted" from OPM's procedures.

Certain positions in all agencies are also excepted. These excepted positions fall into one of three "schedules:"

Schedule A applies to attorneys and certain other non-policymaking positions for which it is impractical to hold competitive examinations.

Schedule B covers positions for which competitive examinations are also impractical but for which noncompetitive examinations may be held, such as for student-trainees.

Schedule C applies to positions that are policymaking or positions that involve a close personal and confidential relationship with key policymaking officials who support the President's political aims and practices.

Applications for a job with an excepted agency or for an excepted service position are generally made directly to the employing agency rather than through OPM.

Benefits

Federal workers receive a full range of fringe benefits: annual leave (two to five weeks a year, depending on length of service), sick leave (10 days a year), nine paid holidays, life insurance, medical insurance, workers' compensation, unemployment compensation, and retirement benefits.

Although federal workers have the right to be represented by unions, the economic benefits they receive are not, for the most part, negotiable.

Promotions

Federal agencies are required to develop merit promotion systems under general OPM guidelines. If an agency's employees are union represented, the agency must develop its merit plan through consultation or negotiation with the union.

When a job vacancy occurs, an agency can fill it in several ways, one of which is by promoting an employee in a lower grade through the agency's merit promotion system. This generally involves posting an "announcement" that the position is vacant and then evaluating the qualifications of the applicants for the position, with the "best qualified" of the applicants being placed on a list from which the selection will be made. The agency's selecting official can choose any of the candidates on the best qualified list. He or she does not necessarily have to select the person at the top of the list or the one with the greatest seniority.

An agency, on the other hand, does not have to fill a position through its merit promotion system. It may fill a position in other ways as well.

- It can reassign an employee to the position.
- It can transfer an employee from another agency.
- It can reinstate a former federal worker with reinstatement rights.
- It can appoint a person from outside the government by obtaining a list of eligible applicants from OPM.

A position may also be filled on a temporary basis (120 days or less), or by promoting an employee in a lower grade through a career promotion, provided the employee obtained his or her current position or grade through competitive procedures and the position provides for a "career ladder" promotion to the grade to which the employee is being promoted. An employee who is not eligible for a career ladder promotion to a higher grade, however, cannot be reassigned, transferred, or reinstated by the agency to a higher grade position or to a position with "higher promotional potential" without giving other employees the opportunity to apply and to be considered for the job under the agency's merit promotion system.

An employee who is not selected for promotion can file a grievance with the agency when there were irregularities in the selection process, but cannot file a grievance if the selection was made from among properly ranked applicants.

If the grieving employee proves that there were irregularities in the selection process, the agency will be required to make a new selection based on proper merit promotion procedures.

Unacceptable Performance and Adverse Actions

A career federal employee in the competitive service who does not meet acceptable levels of work performance may be demoted to a lower grade ("reduction in grade") or be terminated ("removed"), while an employee who engages in misconduct is subject to an "adverse action" proceeding which may result in a reduction in grade, a suspension, a furlough of 30 days or less, or a removal.

Before an agency can take action against an employee for unacceptable performance or misconduct, however, it must follow these procedures:

- If the situation involves unacceptable performance, the agency must counsel the employee and give him or her an opportunity to demonstrate acceptable performance.

* If the agency determines after a period of time that the employee's work performance continues to be unacceptable, or if the situation involves an adverse action, the agency must give the employee 30 days' advance written notice of the action it proposes to take against the employee and specify the reasons for its contemplated action.

* The employee, who is allowed to be represented by an attorney or other representative, must be given a reasonable time to prepare an answer (which must be at least seven days when an adverse action is involved).

* The agency then prepares a written decision specifying the reasons for the action it is taking against the employee.

The employee can challenge the agency's decision in one of two ways: either by filing an appeal with the Merit Systems Protection Board within 20 days, or, if the employee is represented by a union, by filing a grievance. The employee, however, cannot do both.

When an adverse action involves a suspension of 14 days or less, the employee can only file a grievance, either through the union-negotiated grievance system, or, if the employee is not union represented, through the agency's administrative grievance system. A suspension of 14 days or less cannot be appealed to the Merit Systems Protection Board.

An employee in the Senior Executive Service being disciplined because of alleged misconduct can appeal the agency's decision to the Merit Systems Protection Board. When the agency's action involves the employee's removal because of poor work performance, however, the employee has no right to a formal appeal to the Board.

An action against an administrative law judge can be instituted by the employing agency by filing a complaint with the Board. The Board then holds a formal hearing on the complaint.

A person dissatisfied with the Board's decision in any of the situations referred to above can appeal either to the U.S. Court of Claims or to a U.S. Court of Appeals. An appeal to either court must be filed within 30 days of the Board's decision.

Reductions in Force

On occasion, an agency may be required to reduce the number of workers it employs. When faced with a reduction in force ("RIF"), the agency must follow prescribed procedures for laying off its employees.

The agency must first determine the geographic area and positions affected. It then places the affected employees in one of three groups.

Group 1—Career employees who have completed their probationary period.

Group 2—Career employees who have not completed their probationary period and career-conditional employees.

Group 3—Employees with an indefinite status, such as temporary employees and employees serving for a specific term.

Employees in each group are then ranked according to their length of service, with the longest-term employees ranked highest and veterans being ranked ahead of nonveterans. An employee with a current outstanding performance rating receives additional years of credit.

Employees are then laid off, after receiving at least a 30-day notice, in reverse order of their ranking, with the lowest ranked employee in Group 3 being the first laid off and the top-ranked employee in Group 1 being the last.

An employee in Group 1 or 2, but not one in Group 3, has the right to "bump" a less senior employee by taking his or her job if the employee doing the bumping is qualified to do the work, or may "retreat" to a lower grade job that the employee had formerly held.

If there are no jobs for the employee to bump into or retreat to, he or she is laid off and placed on a reemployment priority list. Group 1 employees remain on the list for two years; Group 2 employees for one year. Employees in the "excepted" service generally do not have the right to bump or be placed on a reemployment list.

Employees placed in a lower graded position because of a reduction in force may retain their grades for two years. They then receive the grade of the position they are occupying, but at a within-grade pay step that provides a wage comparable to that received before the reduction in force.

An employee separated from government service because of a reduction in force, or for any other reason for which the employee was not at fault, and who is not entitled to immediate retirement benefits may be eligible for severance pay, which is based on years of service but which cannot exceed one year's basic salary.

Laid-off employees may appeal to the Merit Systems Protection Board if they believe that the agency did not follow required reduction-in-force procedures.

Unions

Federal employees have the right to join and participate in union activities. The Federal Labor Relations Authority (FLRA), an agency similar to the NLRB, but with less overall authority, oversees federal labor relations. Like the NLRB, the FLRA conducts elections to determine whether employees want union representation and processes unfair labor practice complaints.

Agencies and unions are required to negotiate grievance systems covering all matters except those which by law or regulation are excluded from grievance systems. Agencies whose employees are not union represented are also required to provide grievance systems for their workers.

Equal Employment Opportunity

It is unlawful for an agency to discriminate against an employee or applicant for employment because of race, color, religion, sex, national origin, age, or handicap. The following is the procedure employees use for processing complaints of alleged discriminatory practices:

* A federal worker believing that he or she was discriminated against starts the EEO process by contacting the agency's EEO counselor within 30 days of the alleged discriminatory practice.

* If the matter is not resolved, the employee may file a complaint with the agency's EEO director 21 days after the first contact with the counselor, or 15 days after the final interview with the counselor.

* The EEO director investigates the matter and attempts to adjust the matter. If an adjustment is not made, the employee is notified of his or her right to a hearing, or to an agency decision without a hearing.

* If the employee does not reply, or requests a decision without a hearing, the agency makes a decision in the matter.

* Should the employee request a hearing, an examiner from the EEOC conducts a hearing. After the hearing, the examiner prepares a written recommended decision and forwards it to the agency which then makes its final decision in the matter.

* If the employee is not satisfied with the decision, he or she has 20 days to appeal to the EEOC's Office of Review and Appeals, or 30 days to file suit in a federal district court. If the appeal is made to the EEOC, the employee has 180 days after filing the appeal to file a court suit.

More expedited procedures are allowed in cases of alleged age discrimination or violations of the Equal Pay Act. A local EEOC office or an agency EEO counselor can provide more information on these procedures.

The Merit Systems Protection Board can also decide an allegation of unlawful discrimination when it is related to an issue (such as one involving adverse action) that the employee has appealed to the Board.

Prohibited Personnel Practices

Federal agencies are required to observe basic merit principles in the operation of their personnel practices. Among other things federal workers are entitled to fair treatment, protection against arbitrary action or political coercion, and protection against reprisals for lawful disclosures of information, that is, protection for "whistleblowers." These are persons who disclose information about an agency's violation of a law, rule, or regulation; mismanagement; gross waste of funds; abuse of authority; or a substantial and specific danger to public health or safety. A whistleblower, however, is not protected if he or she wrongfully discloses information that is classified, required to be kept secret in the interest of national security, or covered by the federal Privacy Act.

An employee believing that an agency official is violating a merit principle by committing a "prohibited personnel practice"may file a charge with the Special Counsel of the Merit Systems Protection Board. The Special Counsel has the authority to investigate the charge and, if he or she believes a violation has occurred, may recommend that the agency take corrective action. If the agency does not comply, the Special Counsel may request that the Merit Systems Protection Board take action on the matter. The Special Counsel may also file a charge with the Board against an official who has allegedly committed a prohibited personnel practice and recommend that the official be disciplined or removed. An official against whom a charge is filed has essentially the same rights as a person involved in an adverse action, including the right of court appeal.

More information about federal employment can be obtained from OPM and the Merit Systems Protection Board. The addresses for their national offices are:

Office of Personnel Management
1900 E Street, N.W.
Washington, D.C. 20415

Merit Systems Protection Board
1120 Vermont Ave., N.W.
Washington, D.C. 20419

APPENDIX A
State Labor Departments and Human Relations Commissions*

* Not every state has a Human Relations Commission. If you have a civil rights question and your state has no Human Relations office listed here, ask your state's Department of Labor or the federal Equal Employment Opportunity Commission for assistance.

Alabama:
Department of Labor
State Administrative Building,
Suite 651
Montgomery 36130

Department of Industrial
Relations
Industrial Relations Building
Montgomery 36130

Alaska:
Department of Labor
P.O. Box 1149
Juneau 99802

State Commission for
Human Rights
431 West Seventh Avenue,
Suite 101
Anchorage 99501

Arizona:
Industrial Commission
800 West Washington Street
P.O. Box 19070
Phoenix 85005

Civil Rights Division
1275 West Washington Street
Phoenix 85007

Arkansas:
Department of Labor
1022 High Street
Little Rock 72202

California:
Department of Industrial
Relations
State Building Annex
525 Golden Gate Avenue
San Francisco 94102

Department of Fair
Employment and Housing
1201 I Street, Suite 211
Sacramento 95814

Employment and Development
Department
800 Capitol Mall
Sacramento 95814

Colorado:
Department of Labor and
Employment
600 Grant Street, Suite 900
Denver 80203

Civil Rights Commission
1525 Sherman Street, Room 600
Denver 80203

Connecticut:
Labor Department
200 Folly Brook Boulevard
Wethersfield 06109

Commission on Human
Rights and Opportunities
90 Washington Street
Hartford 06106

Delaware:
Department of Labor
820 North French Street
Wilmington 19801

District of Columbia:
Department of Employment
Services
500 C Street, N.W.
20001

D.C. Office of Human Rights
2000 14th Street, N.W., Room 300
20009

Florida:
Department of Labor and Employment Security
2590 Executive Center Circle, East
Suite 206 Berkley Building
Tallahassee 32301

Department of Community Affairs
2571 Executive Center Circle, East
Tallahassee 32301

Georgia:
Department of Labor
254 Washington Street
Atlanta 30334

Hawaii:
Department of Labor and Industrial Relations
830 Punchbowl Street
Honolulu 96813

Idaho:
Department of Labor and Industrial Services
277 North Sixth Street
Boise 83720

Department of Employment
317 Main Street
P.O. Box 35
Boise 83735

Commission on Human Rights
Basement—Statehouse
Boise 83720

Illinois:
Department of Labor
310 South Michigan Avenue
Chicago 60604

Fair Employment Practices Commission
179 West Washington Street, Fourth Floor
Chicago 60602

Indiana:
Department of Labor
100 North Senate Avenue, Room 1013
Indianapolis 46204-2287

Industrial Board
601 State Office Building
100 North Senate Avenue
Indianapolis 46204

Civil Rights Commission
319 State Office Building
100 North Senate Avenue
Indianapolis 46204

Iowa:
Division of Labor Services
100 East Grand Avenue
Des Moines 50319

Iowa Civil Rights Commission
211 East Maple Street
Des Moines 50319

Kansas:
Department of Human Resources
401 Topeka Avenue
Topeka 66603

Commission on Civil Rights
535 Kansas, Fifth Floor
Topeka 66603

Kentucky:
Labor Cabinet
U.S. 127 South
Frankfort 40601

Commission on Human Rights
P.O. Box 60
Louisville 40203

Louisiana:
Department of Labor
1001 North 23rd Street
P.O. Box 94094
Baton Rouge 70804-9094

Office of Labor
5630 Florida Boulevard
P.O. Box 94094
Baton Rouge 70806

Maine:
Department of Labor
20 Union Street, Station No. 54
Augusta 04333

Maine Human Rights Commission
Stevens School Complex, Station No. 51
Augusta 04333

Maryland:
Division of Labor and Industry
Department of Licensing and Regulation
501 St. Paul Place
Baltimore 21202

Department of Human Resources
1100 Eutaw Street
Baltimore 21201

Commission on Human
Relations
Metro Plaza
Mondawmin Mall, Suite 300
Baltimore 21215

Massachusetts:
Executive Office of Labor
One Ashburton Place,
Room 2112
Boston 02108

Department of Labor and
Industry
100 Cambridge Street
Boston 02202

Michigan:
Department of Labor
309 North Washington Square
Lansing 48909

Bureau of Employment Relations
1200 Sixth Avenue
Detroit 48226

Minnesota:
Department of Labor and
Industry
444 Lafayette Road,
Fifth Floor
St. Paul 55101

Department of Human Rights
500 Bremer Tower
Seventh and Minnesota Streets
St. Paul 55101

Mississippi:
Employment Security
Commission
1520 West Capitol
P.O. Box 1699
Jackson 39205

Missouri:
Department of Labor and
Industrial Relations
421 East Dunklin Street
Jefferson City 65101

Montana:
Department of Labor and
Industry
Commissioner's Office
P.O. Box 1728
Helena 59624

Nebraska:
Department of Labor
P.O. Box 94600
550 South 16th Street
Lincoln 68509

Equal Opportunity
Commission
P.O. Box 94934
301 Centennial Mall South,
Fifth Floor
Lincoln 68509

Nevada:
Office of Labor Commissioner
505 East King Street,
Room 602
Carson City 89710

Nevada Equal Rights
Commission
1515 East Tropicana, Suite 590
Las Vegas 89158

New Hampshire:
Department of Labor
19 Pillsbury Street
Concord 03301

New Hampshire Commission
for Human Rights
66 South Street
Concord 03301

New Jersey:
Department of Labor
Labor and Industry Building
John Fitch Plaza
Trenton 08625

Department of Law and
Public Safety
State House Annex
Trenton 08625

New Mexico:
Department of Human Services
PERA Building
P.O. Box 2348
Santa Fe 87503

Human Rights Commission
Bataan Memorial Building,
Room 303
Santa Fe 87503

New York:
Department of Labor
State Office Campus,
Building 12
Albany 12240

Division of Human Rights
2 World Trade Center
New York 10047

North Carolina:
Department of Labor
4 West Edenton Street
Raleigh 27601

North Dakota:
Department of Labor
State Capitol Building
Bismarck 58505

Ohio:
Department of Industrial
Relations
2323 West Fifth Avenue
Columbus 43204

Civil Rights Commission
220 Parsons Avenue
Columbus 43215

Oklahoma:
Department of Labor
1315 Broadway Place
Oklahoma City 73103

Human Rights Commission
Jim Thorpe Building,
Room G-11
Oklahoma City 73105

Oregon:
Bureau of Labor and
Industries
1400 Southwest Fifth Avenue
Portland 97201

Pennsylvania:
Department of Labor and
Industry
Labor and Industry Building
Harrisburg 17120

Pennsylvania Human Relations
Commission
100 North Cameron Street
Harrisburg 17101

Rhode Island:
Department of Labor
220 Elmwood Avenue
Providence 02907

Commission for Human Rights
10 Abbott Park Place
Providence 02903

South Carolina:
Department of Labor
3600 Forest Drive
P.O. Box 11329
Columbia 29211-1329

State Human Affairs
Commission
1111 Belleview Street
Columbia 29211

South Dakota:
Department of Labor
700 Governors Drive
Pierre 57501

State Commission on
Human Rights
State Capitol
Pierre 57501

Tennessee:
Department of Labor
501 Union Building,
Second Floor
Nashville 37219-5385

Tennessee Commission on
Human Rights
208 Tennessee Building
Nashville 37219

Texas:
Department of Labor and
Standards
Box 12157
Capitol Station
Austin 78711

Utah:
Industrial Commission
160 East 300 South
P.O. Box 45580
Salt Lake City 84145-0580

Vermont:
Department of Labor and
Industry
State Office Building
Montpelier 05602

Virginia:
Department of Labor and
Industry
P.O. Box 12064
Fourth Street Office
Building
Richmond 23241-0064

Industrial Commission
1000 DMV Drive
Richmond 23220

Washington:
Department of Labor and
Industries
General Administration
Building
Olympia 98504

State Human Rights
Commission
1601 Second Avenue
Building
Seattle 98101

West Virginia:
Department of Labor
Capitol Complex
1800 Washington Street
East Charleston 25305

State Human Rights
Commission
215 Professional Building
1036 Quarrier Street
Charleston 25301

Wisconsin:
Department of Industry, Labor
and Human Relations
P.O. Box 7946
Madison 53707

Wyoming:
Department of Labor and
Statistics
Herschler Building,
Second Floor
Cheyenne 82002

Fair Employment Commission
Herschler Building,
Second Floor
Cheyenne 82002

APPENDIX B
NLRB and Wage and Hour Division Offices

The following is a list of the locations of the regional and resident offices of the National Labor Relations Board and the regional and field offices of the Wage and Hour Division of the U.S. Department of Labor. These offices, covering all or part of the states indicated, are listed in their respective telephone directories.

State	NLRB Offices	Wage and Hour Offices
Alabama	Atlanta, GA Birmingham, AL New Orleans, LA	Atlanta, GA Birmingham, AL Mobile, AL Montgomery, AL
Alaska	Anchorage, AK Seattle, WA	Seattle, WA
Arizona	Albuquerque, NM El Paso, TX Phoenix, AZ	Phoenix, AZ San Francisco, CA
Arkansas	Little Rock, AR Memphis, TN Nashville, TN	Dallas, TX Little Rock, AR
California	Las Vegas, NV Los Angeles, CA Oakland, CA San Diego, CA San Francisco, CA	Glendale, CA Los Angeles, CA Sacramento, CA San Francisco, CA Santa Ana, CA
Colorado	Denver, CO	Denver, CO
Connecticut	Hartford, CT	Boston, MA Hartford, CT
Delaware	Baltimore, MD Philadelphia, PA Washington, DC	Philadelphia, PA
District of Columbia	Baltimore, MD Washington, DC	Baltimore, MD Philadelphia, PA
Florida	Jacksonville, FL Miami, FL New Orleans, LA Tampa, FL	Atlanta, GA Fort Lauderdale, FL Jacksonville, FL Miami, FL Orlando, FL Tampa, FL

Georgia	Atlanta, GA	Atlanta, GA
	Birmingham, AL	Savannah, Ga
Hawaii	Honolulu, HI	San Francisco, CA
Idaho	Anchorage, AK	Seattle, WA
	Seattle, WA	
Illinois	Chicago, IL	Chicago, IL
	Peoria, IL	Springfield, IL
	St. Louis, MO	
Indiana	Chicago, IL	Chicago, IL
	Cincinnati, OH	Indianapolis, IN
	Indianapolis, IN	South Bend, IN
Iowa	Des Moines, IA	Des Moines, IA
	Minneapolis, MN	Kansas City, MO
	Peoria, IL	
Kansas	Kansas City, KS	Kansas City, MO
Kentucky	Cincinnati, OH	Atlanta, GA
	Indianapolis, IN	Lexington, KY
		Louisville, KY
Louisiana	New Orleans, LA	Baton Rouge, LA
		Dallas, TX
		New Orleans, LA
Maine	Boston, MA	Boston, MA
		Portland, ME
Maryland	Baltimore, MD	Baltimore, MD
	Washington, DC	Hyattsville, MD
		Philadelphia, PA
Massachusetts	Boston, MA	Boston, MA
Michigan	Detroit, MI	Chicago, IL
	Grand Rapids, MI	Grand Rapids, MI
	Milwaukee, WI	
Minnesota	Des Moines, IA	Chicago, IL
	Minneapolis, MN	Minneapolis, MN
Mississippi	Little Rock, AR	Atlanta, GA
	Memphis, TN	Jackson, MS
	Nashville, TN	
	New Orleans, LA	
Missouri	Kansas City, KS	Kansas City, MO
	St. Louis, MO	St. Louis, MO
Montana	Anchorage, AK	Denver, CO
	Seattle, WA	
Nebraska	Kansas City, KS	Kansas City, MO
		Omaha, NE
Nevada	Las Vegas, NV	San Francisco, CA
	Los Angeles, CA	
	Oakland, CA	
New Hampshire	Boston, MA	Boston, MA
New Jersey	Newark, NJ	Newark, NJ
	Philadelphia, PA	New York, NY
		Trenton, NJ
New Mexico	Albuquerque, NM	Albuquerque, NM
	El Paso, TX	Dallas, TX
	Phoenix, AZ	

New York	Albany, NY Brooklyn, NY Buffalo, NY New York, NY	Albany, NY Bronx, NY Brooklyn, NY Buffalo, NY Hempstead, L.I., NY New York, NY
North Carolina	Winston-Salem, NC	Atlanta, GA Charlotte, NC Raleigh, NC
North Dakota	Des Moines, IA Minneapolis, MN	Denver, CO
Ohio	Cincinnati, OH Cleveland, OH	Chicago, IL Cincinnati, OH Cleveland, OH Columbus, OH
Oklahoma	Fort Worth, TX Tulsa, OK	Dallas, TX Tulsa, OK
Oregon	Portland, OR	Portland, OR Seattle, WA
Pennsylvania	Philadelphia, PA Pittsburgh, PA	Harrisburg, PA Philadelphia, PA Pittsburgh, PA
Rhode Island	Boston, MA	Boston, MA Providence, RI
South Carolina	Winston-Salem, NC	Atlanta, GA Columbia, SC
South Dakota	Des Moines, IA Minneapolis, MN	Denver, CO
Tennessee	Atlanta, GA Baltimore, MD Birmingham, AL Little Rock, AR Memphis, TN Nashville, TN Washington, DC	Atlanta, GA Knoxville, TN Memphis, TN Nashville, TN
Texas	Albuquerque, NM El Paso, TX Fort Worth, TX Houston, TX Phoenix, AZ San Antonio, TX Tulsa, OK	Corpus Christi, TX Dallas, TX Fort Worth, TX Houston, TX San Antonio, TX
Utah	Denver, CO	Denver, CO Salt Lake City, UT
Vermont	Boston, MA	Boston, MA
Virginia	Baltimore, MD Washington, DC	Philadelphia, PA Richmond, VA
Washington	Seattle, WA	Seattle, WA
West Virginia	Baltimore, MD Cincinnati, OH Pittsburgh, PA Washington, DC	Charleston, WV Philadelphia, PA

Wisconsin	Des Moines, IA	Chicago, IL
	Milwaukee, WI	Madison, WI
	Minneapolis, MN	Milwaukee, WI
Wyoming	Denver, CO	Denver, CO

APPENDIX C
EEOC Offices

Albuquerque:
505 Marquette, N.W.,
Suite 1105
New Mexico 87101

Atlanta:
75 Piedmont Avenue, N.E.,
Suite 1100
Georgia 30335

Baltimore:
109 Market Place,
Suite 4000
Maryland 21202

Birmingham:
2121 Eighth Avenue, North,
Suite 824
Alabama 35203

Boston:
JFK Building, Room 409-B,
Massachusetts 02203

Buffalo:
28 Church Street,
New York 14202

Charlotte:
5500 Central Avenue,
North Carolina 28212

Chicago:
536 South Clark Street,
Room 930-A
Illinois 60605

Cincinnati:
550 Main Street,
Room 7015
Ohio 45202

Cleveland:
1375 Euclid Avenue,
Room 600
Ohio 44115

Dallas:
8303 Elmbrook Drive,
Texas 75247

Dayton:
200 West Second Street,
Room 608
Ohio 45402

Denver:
1845 Sherman Street,
Second Floor
Colorado 80203

Detroit:
477 Michigan Avenue,
Room 1540
Michigan 48226

El Paso:
109 North Oregon Street,
Texas 79901

Fresno:
1313 P Street,
Suite 103
California 93721

Greensboro:
324 West Market Street,
Room B-27
P.O. Box 3363
North Carolina 27402

Greenville:
211 Century Drive,
Suite 109-B
South Carolina 29607

Houston:
405 Main Street,
Sixth Floor
Texas 77002

Indianapolis:
46 East Ohio Street,
Room 456
Indiana 46204

Jackson:
100 West Capitol Street,
Suite 721
Mississippi 39269

Kansas City:
911 Walnut,
Tenth Floor
Missouri 94106

Little Rock:
320 West Capitol Avenue,
Suite 621
Arkansas 72201

Los Angeles:
3660 Wilshire Boulevard,
Fifth Floor
California 90010

Louisville:
601 West Broadway,
Room 104
Kentucky 40202

Memphis:
1407 Union Avenue,
Suite 502
Tennessee 38104

Miami:
1 Northeast First Street,
Sixth Floor
Florida 33132

Milwaukee:
310 West Wisconsin Avenue,
Suite 800
Wisconsin 53203

Minneapolis:
110 South Fourth Street,
Room 178
Minnesota 55401

Nashville:
Parkway Towers,
Suite 1100
Tennessee 37219

Newark:
60 Park Place,
Room 301
New Jersey 07102

New Orleans:
600 South Maestri Place,
Room 528
Louisiana 70130

New York:
90 Church Street,
Room 1505
New York 10007

Norfolk:
200 Granby Mall,
Room 412
Virginia 23510

Oakland:
1333 Broadway,
Room 430
California 94612

Oklahoma City:
200 Northwest Fifth Street,
Room 703
Oklahoma 73102

Philadelphia:
127 North Fourth Street,
Suite 300
Pennsylvania 19106

Phoenix:
135 North Second Avenue,
Fifth Floor
Arizona 85003

Pittsburgh:
1000 Liberty Avenue,
Room 2038A
Pennsylvania 15222

Raleigh:
178 West Hargett Street,
Suite 500
North Carolina 27601

Richmond:
400 North Eighth Street,
Room 6206
Virginia 23240

San Antonio:
727 East Durango,
Suite 601-B
Texas 78206

San Diego:
880 Front Street,
California 92188

San Francisco:
10 United Nations Plaza,
Fourth Floor
California 94102

San Jose:
280 South First Street,
Room 4150
California 95113

Seattle:
 1321 Second Avenue,
  Seventh Floor
 Washington 98101

St. Louis:
 625 North Euclid Street,
 Missouri 63108

Tampa:
 700 Twiggs Street,
  Room 302
 Florida 33602

Washington, D.C.:
 1717 H Street, N.W.,
  Suite 400
 20006

GLOSSARY

Many words used in describing events occurring in the employer-employee relationship appear in the text of this book. Other terms that have meanings peculiar to employment law, and that are not referred to elsewhere in the book, are defined below.

Absenteeism   Absence from work. Usually refers to excessive absences.

Across-the-board adjustment   Change in the wage rates for workers in a particular group or facility.

Age certificate   A certificate issued by a government or a school official authorizing the employment of a minor.

Agency shop   A contract provision requiring nonunion employees represented by a union to pay the union a sum equal to union dues.

Agent   A person acting in the interests of another, for whose activities the other may be held responsible.

Annuity   Benefits paid to a worker for a given period of time. Usually refers to retirement benefits a worker receives under a pension plan.

Anti-injunction laws   Federal and state laws that limit the authority of courts to issue injunctions in labor disputes.

Antitrust laws   Federal and state laws that protect trade and commerce from unlawful restraints and monopolies. These laws apply mostly to business activities, but sometimes apply to unions.

Area practice   Prevailing wages and benefits in a geographical area.

Assessments   Special charges levied by a union on its members to meet a financial need.

Assignment   (1) An order to a worker to perform a particular task. (2) A pledge by an employee to have part of his or her wages used to pay a debt or used for some other designated purpose.

Association agreement   A collective bargaining agreement that applies to all members of an employer association that negotiates for them jointly with a union.

Automatic renewal A provision in a collective bargaining agreement extending it from year to year in the absence of notice by either party to the agreement to modify or negotiate a new agreement.

Automatic wage progression A system for increasing wages based on length of service.

Award (1) A ruling (decision) by an arbitrator. (2) A favorable determination on an application for Social Security benefits.

Back pay Wages required to be paid to workers who have been unlawfully discharged.

Back-to-work movement Effort by employees opposed to a strike to have striking workers abandon the strike and return to work.

Bartering Arrangement between two or more persons whereby they agree to exchange services instead of money for the work or services they perform for each other.

Base rate An employee's regular rate of pay, excluding any premium pay and fringe benefits. Same as "basic hourly rate."

Bidding An employee's action in seeking a vacant job.

Blacklist (1) A list of union members circulated among employers. (2) A list of employers barred from federal contracts because of their violations of federal contracting requirements.

Blue-collar workers A term generally referring to manual laborers.

Board of inquiry A group of persons appointed to mediate and report to the President in national emergency labor disputes.

Bonus A payment in addition to an employee's regular wage.

Bootleg contract A collective bargaining agreement that attempts to evade working conditions or wages required in other union contracts.

Boycott A refusal to deal with or buy the products of a business as a means of exerting pressure in a labor dispute.

Bureau of Labor Statistics A Bureau in the Labor Department that compiles employment-related statistics, including the Consumer Price Index by which some wage adjustments are determined.

Business agent A paid union official who handles a local union's business matters, organizes workers, negotiates with employers, and generally administers the union's affairs.

"C" cases A term referring to the NLRB's unfair labor practice proceedings.

Call-back pay A guarantee to workers that they will receive a minimum number of hours of work if they are called back to work outside their regularly scheduled working hours.

Call-in pay A guarantee to workers that they will receive a minimum number of hours of work when they are required to report to work. Same as "reporting pay" and "show-up pay."

Captive audience Employees required to attend a meeting during working hours to hear their employer's views on unions.

Card check Checking of a union's authorization cards signed by the employees against the employer's payroll to determine whether the union represents a majority of the employees.

Casual Workers Employees who do not work on a regular basis.

Cease-and-desist order An order by an administrative agency to a union or an employer, or both, to stop engaging in unlawful conduct.

Ceiling Upper limit on wages.

Cessation The termination of a recipient's entitlement to a government benefit.

Challenge An objection by an employer or a union to the right of an employee to vote in an NLRB-conducted election.

Class action A court suit in employment discrimination cases brought on behalf of a group of persons similarly affected by the alleged discriminatory practice, but because the number of persons in the group is so large it is impractical to name them all individually as parties to the suit.

Closed shop An unlawful arrangement between an employer and a union whereby only union members may be hired. A valid union shop agreement must allow workers at least 30 days to join the union.

Coercion (1) Unlawful pressure exerted by an employer to prevent employees from engaging in concerted or union activities. (2) Unlawful intimidation of employees by a union to compel affiliation with the union. (3) Unlawful pressure exerted on an employer by a union to force it to perform an unlawful act.

Company-dominated union A union controlled by the employer.

Compensatory time Time off given instead of overtime pay to employees who work overtime. Compensatory time is generally allowed under the FLSA if time off is given in the same workweek as the one in which the overtime was worked.

Compulsory arbitration Requiring an employer and a union to submit to arbitration any issues they are unable to resolve in negotiations for a collective bargaining agreement. Also sometimes referred to as "interest" arbitration.

Concerted activities Action by two or more employees to improve working conditions or for their mutual aid or protection.

Conciliation A process to help the parties to a labor dispute iron out their differences.

Condonation   An employer's acquiescence in conduct by an employee which normally would be grounds for discipline or discharge.

Consent election   Election held by the NLRB after an informal hearing in which the employer and the union agree on the terms of an election.

Constructive discharge   Treating an employee unfavorably to force him or her to "voluntarily"quit.

Consumer picketing   Picketing a retail store for purposes of urging customers not to patronize the store or not to buy a certain product. If the picketing is in support of a strike against the producer or the supplier, the picketing is legal if it is aimed merely at getting customers not to buy the products of the struck employer. It is unlawful if it is aimed at getting the customers to stop patronizing the store entirely.

Consumer Price Index   The Bureau of Labor Statistics' monthly statistical study which is based on a check of retail prices of selected consumer items and services. *See* Bureau of Labor Statistics.

Contract-bar rules   Rules applied by the NLRB in determining when an existing contract between an employer and a union will bar an election sought by the employees or a rival union.

Contracting out   The action by an employer in which work performed by its workers is transferred to another company.

Cooling-off period   Period during which workers are forbidden to strike.

Cost of living   Relationship of the cost of consumer goods and services to wages.

Cost-of-living adjustment (COLA)   Increase in wages because of an increase in the cost of living.

Counterproposal   An opposing offer made by either a union or an employer following an offer or proposal made by the other party during collective bargaining.

Credit union   An organization composed of and operated by the employees of the same employer to provide its employee-members with a means for investing their money and obtaining loans. Credit unions are chartered under either federal or state law.

Damage suits   Suits that may be brought in federal courts to recover damages for breach of collective bargaining contracts and for violations of prohibitions against secondary boycotts and other unlawful strike action under the National Labor Relations Act.

Davis-Bacon Act   A federal law that fixes the wages that contractors must pay laborers and mechanics engaged in working on federally funded construction projects.

Deadheading   Trucks being driven empty or while not in service.

Decertification   A union's loss of its right to represent employees in collective bargaining.

Deduction   Money withheld from a worker's wages to pay taxes, union dues, or other obligations.

Demotion   The transferring of an employee from a higher to a lower job classification.

Disability Insurance Benefits (DIB)   Social Security disability benefits.

Disestablishment   An order by the NLRB that an employer-dominated union be dissolved.

Docking   Deducting money from a worker's pay for tardiness or absences.

Domestics   Workers employed to perform household duties in private homes.

Double breasted   An employer, usually a construction firm, that operates two separate businesses performing similar work, with the workers of one being union represented while the workers of the other are not represented.

Double time   A pay rate that is twice the worker's straight-time rate of pay.

Downgrade   Demotion to a job with less pay.

Dual union   Situations where a union signs up workers already claimed by another union.

Eligibility   Qualification of an employee to vote in an NLRB election.

Employee Stock Ownership Plan (ESOP)   Arrangement allowing workers to own all or part of the business for which they work.

Entitlement   A condition in which an individual meets all the necessary requirements to receive a government-provided benefit.

Entrance rate   The pay a worker receives when first hired.

Escalator clause   A clause in a collective bargaining agreement requiring a wage adjustment at stated intervals as the cost of living changes.

Escape clause   A provision in a collective bargaining agreement which allows union members a period of time in which they can resign from the union.

Exactions   Payments made for work not done and not intended to be done.

Executive order　A directive by the President or a governor, usually addressed to an administrative agency and affecting a government operation and sometimes the public.

Fact-finding boards　Agencies appointed by the government to determine facts and make recommendations in major labor disputes.

Featherbedding　A contract provision requiring that employees be hired even though their services are not needed.

Federal Unemployment Tax Act (FUTA)　The law requiring employers to pay taxes to fund the unemployment compensation program.

Flexible benefits　The offering of a variety of fringe benefits by an employer to its employees and allowing each worker to select the ones he or she wants with a limit on the number that can be selected. Also sometimes referred to as "cafeteria-style" benefits.

Flextime　A policy in which each worker is allowed to set his or her own work schedule within a general time frame established by the employer.

Free riders　Union-represented workers who refuse to join or pay dues to the union.

Free speech　The right of employers to express their views on unionization to their employees, provided no threats or promises of benefit are made to the employees.

Furlough　A layoff because of lack of work.

Good standing　A union member who is in compliance with all the requirements for membership in the union. Generally means a member whose dues and financial obligations to the union are current.

Goon　A person who engages in violence during a labor dispute.

Green card　A term commonly used to refer to the Alien Registration Receipt Card (INS Form I-151) and Resident Alien Card (INS Form I-551), which are issued by the Immigration and Naturalization Service to lawful permanent resident aliens and which they can use to establish their identity and employment eligibility when they are seeking work.

Grievance　An employee complaint. Under a union contract a grievance is a complaint by the employee that the employer is in violation of some provision of the collective bargaining agreement.

Guard　Plant protection employee.

Hearing　A formal or informal proceeding at which an arbitrator, a hearing officer, an administrative law judge, or a court listens to all sides of the matter before a decision is made.

Hiring hall Place where workers are recruited for work on construction projects.

Holiday *See* Legal Holiday.

Hot cargo Term applied by unions to products of plants employing nonunion workers or to products of employers with which the union has a dispute. A hot-goods or hot-cargo clause under which a union gets an employer to agree not to require its employees to handle or work on hot goods is an unlawful secondary boycott.

Impartial umpire An arbitrator.

Incentive wage plan An arrangement to pay employees extra money for more production.

Incumbent A union currently serving as the employee's bargaining representative.

Independent contractor A person who does a job for a price, decides how the work will be done, can hire others to do the work, and generally depends on profits rather than wages for his or her income.

Independent union A union not affiliated with the AFL-CIO.

Individual contract An agreement between an employer and an employee covering wages and/or working conditions.

Initiation fee Fee required by a union as a condition for a worker to become a union member.

Injunction A court order directing that certain action be taken or not taken.

Inside man A spy placed in a plant as an employee.

Interference Unlawful action which infringes on the right of employees to engage or not engage in union or protected concerted activity.

Interim agreement An agreement setting conditions only for the period from the termination of one contract until a new one is negotiated.

International Labor Organization (ILO) A United Nations agency that proposes improvements in international labor conditions.

Interstate commerce (or "commerce") Trade among the states. The U.S. Constitution gives the federal government the power to regulate interstate commerce. The courts have interpreted this to include the power to regulate activities that also "affect" commerce. The federal government has relied upon this authority as a basis for enacting laws creating the NLRB, EEOC, and FLSA.

Job action Action taken by employees to apply pressure on an employer to force it to accept their demands.

Job analysis Determining a job's requirements by examining its duties and responsibilities.

Job content A job's actual duties and responsibilities.

Job description or classification Evaluation of the nature of the work performed in a job, its relation to other jobs, its responsibilities, and the qualifications needed to do the work.

Job rate Rate of pay for a given job.

Journeyman A craft worker who has completed an apprenticeship and has mastered the type of work he or she was trained to do.

Judicial review Appeal to a court to enforce or set aside an order of an administrative agency.

Jurisdiction (1) Authority of an administrative agency or court to hear and decide a case. (2) A union's authority over certain workers or certain types of work.

Jurisdictional dispute Dispute between two unions over the right to organize a group of workers, or over which union's members are to perform a certain type of work.

Kickback The part of an employee's wages that he or she is forced to refund to the employer or to the person who hired the employee.

Knights of Labor The first national federation of American unions. It was organized in 1869, but no longer exists.

Labor dispute A controversy between an employer and a union.

Labor market A geographic area in which employers seek workers and workers seek employment.

Last-offer ballot A special NLRB-conducted election to give workers involved in a national emergency labor dispute an opportunity to vote on either accepting or rejecting an employer's final offer.

Layoff Usually a temporary separation of an employee from employment because of a lack of work.

Legal holiday A day set apart by law to commemorate a person or an occasion. Employers can require their employees to do any work on a legal holiday that they can require on any other day except for such work as the law may specifically prohibit.

Local union The basic unit of a union organization. The local union has its own constitution and by-laws and elects its own officers. Some unions refer to their locals as lodges.

Longevity Seniority; length of service.

Maintenance of membership A union security agreement that requires employees who are members of a union on a specified date to remain members during the term of the contract.

Make whole Reimbursement to an unlawfully discharged employee for the difference between what he or she would have earned if not discharged and what the employee did earn.

Mandatory injunction A term applied to injunctions the NLRB's General Counsel is required to seek from a court when certain types of unfair labor practices are allegedly being committed.

Master agreement A multiemployer or a national agreement that settles major issues, but does not settle those matters that are left to negotiation between individual companies or plants and local unions.

Maximum hours The number of hours that can be worked at straight-time rates before overtime rates have to be paid.

Medicaid A program providing medical assistance to persons who are eligible for benefits under a welfare program established under the Social Security Act.

Medicare A program providing medical assistance to persons eligible for retirement benefits under the Social Security Act.

Members-only contract A collective bargaining agreement that recognizes a union as the bargaining agent only for those employees who are members.

Merit increase Wage increase based on performance rather than on length of service.

Migratory workers Persons who move regularly from one work site to another, usually doing the same type of work, such as farm workers who follow a harvest from one farm area to another.

Minority union A union that has some members in a bargaining unit but not a majority.

Moonlighting Holding down two or more jobs.

Multiemployer unit A bargaining unit consisting of workers employed by more than one employer.

Multiplant unit A bargaining unit consisting of employees of the same employer but working at separate locations.

National Mediation Board An agency created by the Railway Labor Act to mediate labor disputes in the railroad and air transport industries and to conduct elections to allow workers to choose a bargaining representative.

National Railroad Adjustment Board An agency set up under the Railway Labor Act to settle disputes in the railroad industry arising out of grievances or the application of contracts.

Nepotism Giving jobs, promotions, and other benefits to relatives.

No-raid agreement   An agreement by a union not to try to displace another union as a bargaining agent.

Norris-LaGuardia Act   Federal anti-injunction law that limits the circumstances in which courts can issue injunctions in labor

No-solicitation rule   A company rule prohibiting the solicitation of union dues, memberships, or authorization cards on company time and property.

Old-Age, Survivors and Disability Insurance (OASDI)   The Social Security program providing benefits to retired and disabled workers.

Open shop   A plant, office, or facility in which workers are free to join or not to join a union.

Operating employees   Workers whose activities involve the driving or operation of a bus, truck, or construction equipment.

Order   The directive by an administrative agency or court to an employer or a union to comply with its decision.

Organizational picketing   Picketing an employer in an attempt to induce its employees to join the union.

Outside union   A union seeking to organize and represent workers who are already represented by another union. *See* Incumbent.

Paper local   A local union that is issued a charter by its parent organization before any workers have joined the local.

Past service credits   The credit a worker is given toward a pension for the work he or she performed prior to the creation of the pension plan.

Paternalism   A system in which an employer decides what is best for its workers.

Patrolling   Picketing by employees.

Payment in kind   Remuneration other than money (for example, meals, housing, or reciprocal services) for work performed. *See* Bartering.

Payroll period   The period of time from one payday to the next.

Period of Disability (POD)   A continuous period of at least five months during which a worker is unable to work and is considered to be disabled under the Social Security Act because of a severe physical or mental impairment.

Perquisite ("Perk")   An extra benefit or special consideration usually given to higher levels of management.

Picketing   Advertising by union members with signs or handouts to publicize the existence of a labor dispute.

Piecework   Wages based on the number of units produced rather than on time spent in producing them.

Pirating   Encouraging workers to change jobs by offering them higher wages.

Posting   (1) Announcing a job vacancy. (2) Displaying for workers copies of laws, orders of administrative agencies, or other material that an employer by law must display where it can be seen by its workers.

Premature extension   An attempt by a union and employer to extend an existing collective bargaining agreement prior to its automatic renewal or expiration date to bar a petition for an election filed by the employees or by a rival union.

Premium pay   Pay that a worker receives above his or her straight-time rates, such as overtime pay.

Primary Insurance Amount (PIA)   The amount of monthly Social Security benefits a worker receives when he or she retires or becomes disabled. It is based on the worker's average monthly wage.

Profit-sharing   An arrangement under which a worker receives a share of the employer's profits.

Protected class   Any of the classes of persons protected from job discrimination under equal employment opportunity laws.

Protected concerted activity   Activity that the National Labor Relations Act allows employees to engage in without interference from an employer or union.

"R" cases   NLRB representation (election) cases. "RC" indicates a union-filed petition for election; "RD" a decertification petition; "RM" an employer-filed petition.

Railway Labor Act   A federal law providing procedures for the settlement of disputes between the railroads, the airlines, and the unions representing their employees.

Rank and file   Union members who are not officers.

Rat   A stronger word for "scab."

Rate range   The pay range from minimum to maximum for a given job.

Recognition   An employer's act in accepting and dealing with a union as its employees' bargaining representative.

Recognition picketing   Picketing an employer to force it to recognize the union.

Red circle   A contract provision allowing an employer to pay wages higher than the contract provides for certain positions.

Reinstatement   Returning a job to an unlawfully discharged worker.

Remedial order   An order by an administrative agency to an employer or a union to take corrective action for engaging in unlawful conduct.

Reopening clause A clause in a collective bargaining agreement providing for the reopening of the contract for renegotiations during the term of the contract.

Replacements Workers hired to do the work of strikers.

Representation proceeding *See* "R" cases,

Representative payee A person designated by the Social Security Administration to receive a beneficiary's monthly benefits when such action appears in the beneficiary's best interests.

Restraint and coercion Action by an employer or union that unlawfully hinders the right of employees to engage in, or not engage in, union or concerted activity.

Roving pickets Pickets who follow a struck employer's trucks.

Runaway shop A plant or an operation that has been moved so the employer can avoid bargaining with a union.

Runoff election Second employee election directed by the NLRB when three or more choices were presented to the employees in the first election and none of the choices received a majority of the votes. A runoff election is usually limited to the two choices receiving the greatest number of votes in the first election.

Saving clause A provision in a contract that if any part of the contract is held illegal the rest of the contract will remain binding on the parties.

Scab A term striking union members use to refer to nonstriking workers.

Scale The rate of pay union-represented workers receive.

Schism An internal split in a union resulting in one group breaking away and forming another union.

Seasonal workers Workers hired regularly each year but for only part of the year.

Self-employment Work that an individual does for clients or customers rather than for an employer.

Self-organization Employee action in forming a union.

Seniority Preference given to employees in promotions or pay based on their length of service.

Service Contract Act A federal law fixing the wages that employers providing services to the government must pay their employees.

Settlement agreement A term usually applied when parties to a legal dispute agree to compromise their differences to avoid further litigation.

Set-up man/woman A worker who makes adjustments on machinery for the machine's operator.

Severance pay   A payment to a worker who is being terminated.

Shadowing   Keeping a person under surveillance.

Shape-up   Selecting casual workers from a group or pool of workers.

Share-the-work plan   Plan in which when work falls off, the available work is spread among all the workers to avoid a layoff.

Sheltered workshop   A nonprofit workplace employing handicapped workers.

Shift   An employee's regularly scheduled period of working hours. Usually refers to an operation where two or more groups of workers performing the same work have different working hours.

Shift differential   A premium pay that a worker on a shift other than a day shift receives in compensation for the inconvenient working hours.

Shop steward   Person designated by a union to present grievances of fellow workers to a foreman or supervisor.

Showing of interest   The employee support a union must have in a bargaining unit and which it must show to the NLRB before the NLRB will process the union's election petition.

Sit-down strike   A strike in which the employees refuse to leave the employer's premises.

Situs   The location of a labor dispute. Also a test used by the NLRB to determine whether a union is engaging in an unlawful secondary boycott.

Slowdown   A form of strike in which the employees continue to work but at a slower pace.

Soldiering   Deliberately working at a slower pace.

Sole bargaining representative   A union representing all employees in a bargaining unit as their exclusive bargaining representative.

Speedup   Quickening the work pace.

Statute of limitations   A provision in most laws that bars legal action on a claim or dispute if the required action (e.g., filing a complaint or charge with an agency or a court) is not taken within a specified period of time.

Straight-time pay   Regular or basic hourly rate of pay.

Stranger picketing   Picketing by persons who are not employees of the picketed employer.

Straw boss   A subforeman.

Stretch out   Increasing an employee's work quotas.

Strikebreakers   A term used by union members to refer to persons who accept work that had been performed by striking employees.

Struck work   Work performed by a company for an employer whose employees are on strike.

Subcontracting   Farming out part of a company's work to another company.

Submission agreement   Agreement of the parties to submit a dispute to an arbitrator.

Subsistence allowance   Payment of a worker's expenses while he or she travels on company business.

Successor company   An employer who takes over another's business.

Superseniority   Seniority granted by contract to certain employees in addition to the seniority they have because of their length of service. Union stewards are sometimes given superseniority.

Supplemental unemployment benefits   Employer-provided payments to laid-off employees to supplement their government-provided unemployment benefits.

Surveillance   Keeping a watch on employees to detect union activity.

Sweat shop   A low-paying operation with poor working conditions.

Sympathetic strike   Strike called to influence the outcome of a strike at another employer's facility.

Take-home pay   The actual amount in a paycheck after all deductions are made.

Temporary employee   A worker hired with the understanding that his or her employment will not be permanent.

Tenure   Status given an employee, usually after serving a probationary period, assuring the employee of the permanency of his or her job.

Termination   (1) The permanent separation of an employee from a job either by the employer discharging the employee or by the employee quitting. (2)Cessation of the payment of a government-provided benefit when the beneficiary is no longer entitled to receive that type of benefit.

Three-year rule   NLRB rule that the first three years of a valid collective bargaining agreement will bar a petition for an election by a rival union or any attempt to decertify the union.

Traveling card   A card issued by a local union to a member who will be working in another area under the jurisdiction of another local union.

Turnover   The number of workers who quit or are terminated in a given period of time.

Two-tier wages A pay system that allows an employer to pay lower wages to recently hired workers than it paid to new employees hired in the past.

Umpire (1) An arbitrator. (2) An official who hears and decides workers' compensation cases.

Unauthorized strike A strike by a local union without the parent international union's consent.

Unconditional offer Stated willingness of a union to call off a strike without any qualifications.

Underemployed Persons who work in low-wage jobs or work less than full-time who would like to work more or at better paying jobs.

Under-the-table pay Payments to a worker for which no records are kept.

Unfair employment practice Discrimination in employment based on race, color, religion, sex, or national origin.

Unfair labor practice (ULP) Employer or union workplace conduct that the National Labor Relations Act prohibits.

Unfair list Names of employers publicized by unions as "unfair" because of disputes the unions have with them.

Unilateral action Action taken by one party to a collective bargaining agreement without consulting the other concerning a matter that is negotiable. Such action is usually an unfair labor practice.

Union insignia Buttons or other signs worn by employees to indicate that they are union members.

Union label A mark placed on goods indicating that they have been made by union-represented workers.

Vacation Authorized annual period of leave.

Vested rights Rights of workers to pension or profit-sharing plan benefits upon satisfying the conditions in the plan for receiving benefits.

Wage Payment for the performance of work or services.

Wage and hour law The Fair Labor Standards Act.

Waiver Surrendering of a claim.

Walk out A strike.

Welfare plan A plan that provides insurance and other benefits to employees and their families.

White-collar workers Generally refers to employees who work in offices.

Wildcat strike A strike by employees without their union's consent.

Work restriction Union-imposed limitation on the kind or amount of work union members will perform.

Work time The time spent by employees for which they are entitled to be paid under the Fair Labor Standards Act.

Work-to-rule Doing no more work than the minimum required.

Yellow-dog contract An unlawful agreement under which an employee agrees not to join a union while working for the employer.

Zipper clause A contract clause that seeks to prevent any further negotiations for the term of the contract.

INDEX

About the Author

James W. Hunt, a Washington, D.C., lawyer, is a former attorney with the National Labor Relations Board and was labor law counsel for the United States Chamber of Commerce. He is presently a federal Administrative Law Judge.